Leading
Constant
Change

Leading Constant Change

A practical framework for making change happen

Philip Webb

PEARSON

Harlow, England • London • New York • Boston • San Francisco • Toronto • Sydney • Auckland • Singapore • Hong Kong
Tokyo • Seoul • Taipei • New Delhi • Cape Town • São Paulo • Mexico City • Madrid • Amsterdam • Munich • Paris • Milan

Pearson Education Limited
Edinburgh Gate
Harlow CM20 2JE
United Kingdom
Tel: +44 (0)1279 623623
Web: www.pearson.com/uk

First published 2015 (print and electronic)

Pearson Education is not responsible for the content of third-party internet sites.

ISBN: 978–1-292–01747–1 (print)
        978–1-292–01749–5 (PDF)
        978–1-292–01750–1 (ePub)
        978–1-292–01748–8 (eText)

British Library Cataloguing-in-Publication Data
A catalogue record for the print edition is available from the British Library

Library of Congress Cataloging-in-Publication Data
A catalog record for the print edition is available from the Library of Congress

10 9 8 7 6 5 4 3 2 1
18 17 16 15 14

Cover design by Rob Day

Print edition typeset in 10.25 pt Frutiger LT Pro by 3
Printed by Ashford Colour Press Ltd, Gosport

NOTE THAT ANY PAGE CROSS REFERENCES REFER TO THE PRINT EDITION

To my two wonderful daughters, Sophie and Maria, who are about to start their own exciting journey into the world of work and constant change.

With special thanks to Vanessa Daniel, who inspired, cajoled and encouraged me to write this book.

Contents

Part 2 The 15 steps to leading constant change 71

About the author

Philip Webb started his career as a technical specialist working for IBM UK. He spent the 1980s experiencing a period of significant technological change, which was just the start of the revolution that included the advent of the internet.

His first business, selling and supporting computer mainframes, grew from start to £6.7 million in just five years. After selling this business in 1996, he operated a joint venture with BDO until 2002, offering consultancy in various forms. Between 2002 and 2006 he mentored some 137 pre-start businesses in a high growth support scheme, and subsequently started the TAM UK business, which focuses on the Team Action Management programme developed by Albert Humphrey.

He is a former president of Derbyshire Chamber of Commerce (1995) and CBI East Midlands regional councillor (1995–7). A staunch supporter of SME businesses, he co-authored *The Small Business Handbook* (FT Pearson) and *Small Businesses Built to Last* (FT Pearson). He continues his career today delivering the Team Action Management framework to both private sector companies and public sector organisations in the UK.

Outside work, he is a qualified open water PADI licence holder, keen motorcyclist and clay pigeon shooter, and public speaker at various events across the UK.

Acknowledgements

I would like to acknowledge the people and organisations who have been instrumental in both the content and the construction of this book: John Bradley, ex-director of Kier Group; David Clarkson, director of Armstrong Watson; David Hancock, who authored and supports the accompanying website; Albert S. Humphrey, author of the Team Action Management programme; Mark Steed, director of FM Solutions; TAM UK, the company that owns this programme's intellectual property, and its delivery teams; the University of Sheffield, which used the Team Action Management framework in a Post Graduate Certificate in Strategic Change Management; and finally the various clients who have provided testimony to the working of Team Action Management.

Publisher's acknowledgements

The publishers are grateful to TAM UK for permission to reproduce copyright material.

Gratitude is also expressed to the clients of Team Action Management for permission to reproduce their comments: John Wybrant, Mark Steed, Andrew Frith, Paul Dickson and Jennifer Wilson.

In some instances we have been unable to trace the owners of copyright material and we would appreciate any information that would enable us to do so.

Foreword

Since the beginning of time, we have witnessed constant change in our ability to live, eat, grow communities and cities and in people and machine connectivity. Since the world's first telegraph was sent, the first crackly phone call was made, in an incredibly short space of time we now have over half the world's population connected to the internet.

The pace of change, fuelled by both technology and population explosion in the last century has taken us all on a breathtaking journey of change.

Our ability both to understand this change and react to it in our businesses however is lagging behind, and will lead to the certain failure of those businesses who fail to respond.

Our management style is one of command and control, with a hierarchy of management teams and directors who are in post supposedly to control our businesses.

In the last 30 years, company executive managers and directors have been trained and supported by financial legislation to REDUCE risks, drive out process variances and as a consequence reduce the ability of a company to react and change to its rapidly changing markets and customers.

The recession of 2008 started an eye-watering list of large brand failures as the straightjacket management style came home to roost, and we saw household names go bust.

In the next ten years, we need to confront the fact that our command and control management style is no longer fit for purpose in this information age where our staff and customers have never been so educated and so connected.

The need to include our staff in our planning process which we glibly call 'engagement' is failing to get meaningful results, and is in many cases paying lip service to the idea of involving people to gain performance. Effective management of risk must involve all our people, not just those at the top of the pyramid.

It is not performance we are now fighting for, it is the very survival of our businesses in the few years ahead, and if you believe you are in a strong position and this won't affect your company, then the writing is already on the wall for your eventual failure.

Using a proven framework to actively utilise and invite the brains and ideas of all of your people to act in one programme to better the company, is an ideal position that few have achieved.

This book outlines in detail and provides you with both the thinking and the practical method of doing just that.

Imagine a repeatable management driven framework that delivers practical results, backed by an impressive psychological system, which has been translated into a plain and simple step- by- step guide for your success.

This book blows the whistle on an archaic approach to managing, which if we are to succeed will need to be replaced quickly.

Replaced not with the latest fad or management idea, but with a practical sensible and achievable system for delivering results. This framework has been around a few decades as one of the best kept secrets, from the same team that invented the SWOT analysis and the STAKEHOLDER concept.

Brought to you now, in a website supported book, this will seriously challenge your thinking, but simultaneously provide you with the working solution.

Dr Ian Peters
Chief Executive, Chartered Institute of Internal Auditors

Introduction

Before you start reading this book, I need to warn you that in your organisation, right now, there is an invisible killer.

The killer lurks in your buildings, it feeds on people's fears, and spreads like a virus – passed from one person to another, one team to another. Left unchecked, it can kill your organisation as surely as a company liquidator.

It takes an uninvited seat at your board meetings, rudely intrudes on your management meetings, and becomes highly active in meeting areas such as vending machines and canteens. Its effect can be devastating. It overcomes logic, defies explanations and laughs in the face of change. It can sabotage your best-laid plans with ease, and take away the efforts of even your best people at a single stroke.

It can be beaten, but first you will need to identify it, and then plan to contain it. Once you have, you will need to stay vigilant, and never allow it to take back control.

The killer has a name: it is called **metathesiophobia**. It's defined in the dictionary as 'a persistent, abnormal, and unwarranted fear of change'.

And yet, according to recent research, creating and implementing 'change initiatives' is the number-one priority for directors of organisations of all sizes.

I have previously written about start-up and early-stage companies, focusing on creating practical plans for growth and success. From my own experience in the last decade it has become very clear that businesses of all sizes and shapes need to behave like an early-stage company at least a couple of times a year, in order to respond to the enormous changes that beset our markets and organisations every 6–12 months.

Fortunately for me, almost at the very start of my business life, I was taught the secret of how to manage constant change and overcome metathesiophobia. It's a technique that I have used in a career that now spans over 25 years – as director and owner of several businesses, mentor and consultant to several hundred others. That secret has already been passed on to a small number of very successful business owners, directors and managers, and put to good use in both large international corporates such as Cadbury, Kier Group and Roche, as well as in small private businesses and a handful of councils in the public sector.

Due to the nature of the secret and the success it has brought, it has largely remained private knowledge, as most of the organisations believe that it gives them an advantage in their markets over that of their competition. This book will now disclose that secret framework to you. It will outline the steps used by many successful businesses, large and small. It is a framework that has been used by some executives to make their personal fortunes, and by others to create household-name companies.

Most of you will not have heard of it. You will all know its stable-mate, the technique that was created by the same research team at the same time – the widely used management tool called SWOT (Strengths, Weaknesses, Opportunities and Threats). Yet the programme that can transform businesses and create a framework for positive and profitable change remains a mostly hidden gem.

In this book, I will disclose how the framework works, tell you how to use it, and how to achieve results – fast. I have also created a support website for your exclusive use as readers of this book.

Managing change

Over my own 25 years in business, I have often observed managers and executives who are competent in dealing with organisational change, and are able to lead and enthuse people and teams. Even when things look pretty bleak, people follow them and engage with their ideas. These are the people who are able to create teams of superior and higher performance, even when things are constantly changing around them.

I have also worked with CEOs who have ignored the winds of change. They tried to maintain the status quo and eventually failed to react in time when the markets shifted, so their customers moved to their competition, or to a different product or business model. In many cases these companies failed, or were swallowed up by other companies, or were radically restructured, or were simply downsized to a smaller organisation.

So managing and leading constant change has its rewards and its consequences for those who are in the position of delivering the outcomes.

Without doubt, the pace of change in the world is accelerating and quantum changes are happening every year in the markets. If you don't think that's true, then you are on the 'likely to fail' list already.

> *"When the rate of change outside exceeds the rate of change inside, the end is in sight."*
>
> JACK WELCH, CEO, GENERAL ELECTRIC

No longer do we have – or even need – three-year or five-year business plans. They will certainly be out-dated by the end of the first year. What we do need is a living document that has a three-year horizon, but with quarterly or six-monthly revisions, and an understood repeatable process and framework for revising it.

So just how do you set about managing and leading constant change? Surprisingly, for something so very important, there is no definitive approach. Why is it not taught in our schools and universities? Why is this not a basic curriculum subject, like maths and languages?

In my business life I have worked with hundreds of organisations – from both the private and public sector, and from the very largest of companies right down to the smallest start-up companies, or smaller departments within organisations. In every case, every leader asks the same questions:

- How can I put together the very best business plan, which allows for constant change?
- How can we develop and move forward with the fullest support of all the staff?
- How do I lead constant change?

This book will provide you with a real-life framework so that you can initiate, control and then manage rapid and constant change within your business. It is a framework that you can then apply, and repeat, whenever you need it.

This framework is a powerful antidote to metathesiophobia. It is a framework that was originally developed by Albert Humphrey, who also created the SWOT analysis. The intellectual property to this framework, and also the SWOT analysis, passed to me and my company on Albert's death in 2005, and I have been delivering it to a wide selection of clients ever since.

This book shares with you the principles and applications of the framework for leading constant change. It will show you how the framework works and why, and provide you with all the resources to lead change in your business.

In short, the time is right to share the secret that was taught to me.

How to use this book

This is an active book, with interactive support and tools that you can find on the book's own website (**www.managingconstantchange. co.uk**) or even by contacting me direct (**Philip@tamplc.com**).

Each chapter includes a list of key points at the beginning and a list of action points at the end. I also use stories and examples drawn from my own experience, to show you how to set up this framework and how to use it for your own success.

 www.managingconstantchange.co.uk

Wherever you see this icon it means that there is web content available, to download from the book's website for your own private use. All the online content is free of charge. In exchange for your email address, you can download the forms, tools and comment files to use freely in your own organisation. You will also be sent free updates, blogs and comments, to provide continued support along the way.

Other icons are used throughout the book to highlight key points:

 Thinking point

 Research point

So your journey is about to begin, supported by a live website, a team of real change professionals behind the scenes, and a book that will share with you a proven approach to leading constant change. Enjoy your path to success!

part one

Setting the scene for change

So why do I need to change?

Key points in this chapter:

- How four critical factors drive change in your business and also in your personal world as a consumer:
  - technology
  - population
  - markets
  - people.
- How you can use this knowledge to drive your business.

To get the most from the change framework in this book, I want you to open your mind a little, to appreciate the external factors that initiate and drive changes around you. It is these factors that ultimately must convince you that you must also change – or die. By the end of this chapter, you will understand the key drivers of change, and how you need to use this understanding to help you to form ideas and plans for your own organisation.

So, why do you need to change? The simple answer is that you need to change in order to survive. In the world of work, this applies to the changes in the way you do business, the route to market, your customers and their expectations, and of course your shareholders and stakeholders and their expectations of your performance.

"Develop or die."

ROBERT F. STEWART, STANFORD RESEARCH INSTITUTE

Changes to the social environment

'Change' is simply a function of events stemming from the passing of time and moving circumstances.

'You have to move with the times' is a common saying, but what does it really mean?

In day-to-day living we give as little thought to incremental, daily or personal change as we do to the very act of breathing. However, in business or with groups of people it is different. Here, the apparent need or desire to consult and gain common agreement makes the managing of any event much trickier, especially if it involves changes that impact negatively on some individuals. I will show you later the reasons why getting groups of people to plan changes is so difficult (Chapter 2).

So what aspects of life are changing the fastest, and what is the impact on you and your organisation?

There are two main drivers behind the majority of all aspects of change in both our personal and business lives. These two primary drivers of change are technology and population. Of course, there are many others that I am sure you may identify, but they are secondary drivers or consequences of these two primary ones (this chapter looks later at the secondary drivers of markets and people).

Technology is changing

It took 38 years for the number of radio owners to reach 50 million. It took 16 years for 50 million people to own a personal computer. It took just 4 years for 50 million people to become users of the internet. Three years after that, in 2000, this figure had reached 360 million – and don't forget the internet was only available for public use since the early 1990s. By 2012 it was estimated that 2.4 billion people had access to the internet, which represented over one-third of the population of the entire planet.

We have moved way past the age where technology was described as a productivity tool; it is now a way of life, woven into nearly everything we do. Today's children are the 'internet generation' – they have never known life without a personal computer and internet connectivity.

 Generation Z refers to people born between the mid-1990s and 2010 – the digital natives who have grown up in a digital world. To find out more about these media multitaskers, see: **www.grailresearch.com/pdf/ContenPodsPdf/ Consumers_of_Tomorrow_Insights_and_Observations_About_ Generation_Z.pdf**

The uses of the internet are exploding into almost every area of living, and not just in the workplace – from home automation and internet-monitored health, to different ways of interacting with customers. By the end of 2013 internet consumer transactions accounted for around 10 per cent of all retail sales in the UK, with an average weekly spend of just over £650 million.

Channel shifting, which is where a business decides to use technology to automate interactions with the customer, can reduce costs and transform the way we all operate.

 What channels do you currently use for your products and services, and how could you deliver for less, using an alternative technology-driven channel?

Population and demographics are changing

Another result of advances in technology is the way it is redefining entire lifestyles, leading to a significant ability to live longer and in better health. The world population has therefore grown, and is still growing exponentially in a rather startling way: from just over 1 billion only a hundred years ago to an estimated 7.1 billion in 2013 (with a rise of 1 billion in less than 13 years). The next billion after that is estimated in 2025, only 12 years later, and it is thought that the world population will reach around 11 billion in 2050.

With such a huge increase in demand for resources, technology has responded with innovations and inventions that change the way we think and behave. So change is being driven by population increases and the movement of people around the planet, and technology is constantly developing to cater for the increasing consumer take-up and ever-growing demand.

It is these two major factors – huge population increases and innovative technology changes – that are the consequential building blocks of other drivers of change, having by far the most profound impact on our lives in the decades ahead.

As a result of these changes in population and technology, there has been a shift in attitudes. The culture of society and workforces has shifted rapidly over the last 20 years, and people now have very different expectations and possibilities.

People are now seeking more meaning from their work and from their lives.

- People in far-flung exploited parts of the world now have a voice, a stage and an audience, largely enabled by technology and the internet.
- Customers, informed by the increasing transparency and availability of information, are demanding that organisations behave more responsibly and sensitively.
- Increasing numbers of people are fed up with the traditionally selfish character of corporations and organisations and the way they conduct themselves.
- The growing transparency of corporate behaviour in the modern world is creating a new accountability – a move away from the organisations that hitherto have protected the self-interests of the few to the detriment of everyone and everything else.

- Today, many people – staff, customers, everyone – demand and expect change.

Your markets are changing

It is of course a natural reaction to sit back at this stage and say, 'Well, I can't do anything about the technology, even if I did understand it, and I certainly can't do anything about the world population, so what's the point of thinking about it?'

But as a leader in any organisation it is essential that you know about the key factors in the environment in which you provide goods or services, if you are to succeed over the medium term or even the short term.

If you are the captain of a ship, sailing the open seas, you would be expected to know what the capabilities of the ship were, and to steer a course appropriately. But then, when you were under way, you would also be expected to know when a storm was due, or when there might be heavy winds or rain, and then to take action to plot the safest route and timing for your ship for the benefit of your cargo and people.

So in the world of business, or an organisation providing public services, you need to have some idea of things happening in the world around you. To do this, you need to conduct an intelligence-gathering exercise, so that you can then begin to look at how you can respond, how you plan, and what your options are. A simple planning and audit tool you can use is called PEST – Political, Economic, Social and Technological analysis.

 *PEST analysis*

PEST analysis

Download the template and then think about which approach is best for you.

- If you complete this exercise on your own, you will have one view and one intellect, providing a result that you may not find too surprising!
- If you involve others, you could include other directors or managers, technical people (with specialist knowledge), stakeholders, customers and suppliers – the list goes on. You will then have a very broad range of views, facts, knowledge, ideas and interpretations, and so will be able to produce a detailed PEST analysis that will inform and help you.
- Why don't you use this exercise as a team-building opportunity, or a strategic review with your suppliers, customers or stakeholders?

Your people are changing

This section is not about the stereotypical 'perfect' employee – that ideal person with a crafted job description, a set of agreed time based objectives, a fully integrated training and development plan, and a perfectly formatted personnel file that charts progress, achievements, promotions and the sparks of genius that make them top performers. Instead, we need to consider real people – the ones you actually employ.

These are the people who come from varied backgrounds, with differing views, and fluctuating levels of energy and ability. They may have been promoted because they were great at the technical tasks, but they have failed to receive proper formalised management training and so now they simply do their best. These are people who succumb to pressures and stresses, and as a result may do things that you and your business wished they didn't. They make up the great workforce that you employ and attempt to manage on a daily basis: they are your people.

Back in the sixteenth century, the Italian statesman Machiavelli wrote:

"And it ought to be remembered that there is nothing more difficult to take in hand, more perilous to conduct, or more uncertain in its success, than to take the lead in the introduction of a new order of things. Because the innovator has for enemies all those who have done well under the old conditions, and lukewarm defenders in all those who have the law on their side, and partly from the incredulity of men, who do not readily believe in new things until they have had long experience of them."

NICCOLÒ MACHIAVELLI, *THE PRINCE*, 1513

Machiavelli was describing simple human nature in periods of change. He knew that people are more comfortable sticking to the 'old' – the tried and trusted. They are reluctant to adopt the 'new' and only give it passing support until such time as they trust the new and adopt it. Until then, they give lukewarm support, just in case it succeeds, so then they can claim that they supported it all along! Sound familiar?

The inertia when having to do something new, even knowing what that something is, often keeps companies sticking to the old and proven solutions that have brought success in the past. A state of inertia among executives is often linked to a fear of failure, and a fear of the power structure that directs the company. Their sense of 'fair play' is undermined (or maybe it never existed) and this means that impartial decisions are difficult to make. And so the necessary commitment to change from the management team may not materialise.

In the twentieth century business activities became simply a family of 'programmes and projects' of differing importance, priority and completion-due dates. In the twenty-first century the speed of externally driven change has made it even more critical for businesses to be managed by components and projects, with the ability to flex and react quickly. Today, increasing competition in your markets requires you to strive always to be the very best – with so-called 'world-class' operations both in people and business systems.

CREATING EXCELLENCE

World-class systems can be developed by management consultants and software people, but who is going to produce world-class people? Do you hire them or do you create them? Since companies are run and staffed by 'normal' people', the best bet is to create them. But much human sacrifice is needed to attain excellence or become world class, so are your people seriously ready to become excellent, and do they really want to?

Just how do you get your company's employees to embrace the excellence concept?

- How do you get them to act always for the best for the company?
- How do you encourage them to give their all to keep customers satisfied?
- How do you turn them into lean workers?

What you need to do is to convince the employees that this is exactly what they want to do, because such attitudes do not come naturally to most people, no matter where they are in the organisation.

Motivation theorists have come up with many ideas about how people can be urged to take up responsibility, and willingly commit themselves to do the changes required of them by the company. Some of these theories have also been developed into management systems that have been recommended and tried out in practice – with varying success.

To understand why so many management tools have been dropped after just a few years (because they have not dealt with the real problems of the companies), you need to understand two important factors that obstruct this type of human behaviour in organisations.

- **People naturally fear change, and require easily understood rules to help them.** Remember that it is normally 'ordinary' and not 'extraordinary' people that you deal with in your business.

Your employees are not always 'ideal' workers who have the knowledge, interpersonal skills, personal drive and initiative that are needed to operate your sophisticated management systems.

- **People change more slowly than the processes you create**. If you do not allow for a gap between the implementation of the process and the catching up by the human employees, you will have serious problems in successfully implementing the change project.

Of course, if people were not affected by some common traits of human nature – such as playing politics, building up power structures and bringing outside cultural and social inequalities into the company – then the amount of successful business ventures might increase considerably.

> *"As a consequence, managers have inter-departmental and inter-professional conflicts; workers do not trust management, and management think the workers are lazy and unwilling to understand the company's problems. Such factors add to any ordinary inter-personal conflicts that might exist, and they create an atmosphere of fear and mistrust which degenerate the motivation and commitment to change."*

FRANK SONNENBERG, *MANAGING WITH A CONSCIENCE*, 2011

According to marketing expert Frank Sonnenberg, an atmosphere of trust results in more commercial activity, more loyal customers, higher morale among the employees, less absenteeism and higher profit margins. This is because people who trust each other share information and listen to one another. It is also more likely that they will accept any criticism, rather than becoming defensive when receiving feedback. They will then not waste time playing politics, but instead feel comfortable about raising new ideas to be discussed. In this way they can help each other as they all try to change the business for the better.

So it seems logical that what a company needs to do is to create an atmosphere of trust – but how?

Changing the mental programming and the value systems of workers and managers takes time. Resistance to these types of personal changes are even stronger than the normal disagreement over how things should be done. However, by consciously trying to introduce processes that have a positive effect on bringing the business teams closer together, trust can be achieved.

What does this mean for your business?

The problem with a change project is that it has to operate within the day-to-day work of an organisation.

- Companies take care of business before anything else.
- Survival in business depends on doing real work and making profits.
- The competitive situation is so tough that other things must not interfere with what is being done, and even less upset the daily functioning of a company.
- Business results are the first priority.

Finding a management system that can acknowledge and address these issues is not easy. This is especially true because organisations are social systems, and in social systems people interact.

The closer people work together, the easier the communication becomes. When people work together they can decide what is important and create a 'group spirit' – a sense of belonging that easily transfers to the entire company. But nothing will be done if it interferes with the daily business. This means that the 'normal' work must go parallel with any change project. The two have to be integrated, so the strategic planning must then take both into consideration at the same time – you cannot plan for one without the other.

So all this means that you have to introduce changes as you go along in your everyday routine. Learning by doing – on the job.

From my experience over the last 25 years helping companies to change, I have come to the conclusion that successful management is based upon getting ordinary, real people to participate directly in the real decision-making process. It is about taking strategic actions to manage the real work of a company as well as the intended change, made in an atmosphere of trust and fair play. Furthermore, companies need a guiding tool that helps them systemise the work and control its implementation.

In fact a company can change successfully by using management theories and techniques that are already known to most managers. What is needed, though, is to weave these techniques together in a way that gives them a new purpose – which is why you need the framework in this book.

Are you ready for change?

Before we move on to the practical steps to change, you need to consider how ready you are to change. How open or accepting are you, as an individual, to move with the times? And how ready is your team for change? Even before a change is announced, it is possible for you, as the leader, to anticipate reasons why people might resist.

Complete the following two checklists to see where your pressure points are, and where there might be any blockages on your road to leading constant change.

 Planning to move forwards

Do you plan to move forwards?

	OFTEN	QUARTERLY	ANNUALLY	RARELY	NEVER
How often do you review the markets in which you operate?					
Do you have a regular senior team review of the market forces?					
How often do you analyse your competition?					
Do you review your business plan and financial forecasts?					
How often do you take training, or attend seminars or workshops?					
Do you encourage your team to learn new skills?					
Do you ask your customers what they want next year?					
Does technology seem too complex for you?					
Do you review your customers' markets and pressures?					
Do you know what your customers' biggest pressure is in their markets?					
Do you formalise your approach to development work within your organisation?					

So how did you do? Lots of 'often' ticks makes you a forward-looking manager, able to look ahead, understand the likely changes and anticipate the benefits for your organisation. If you have ticked a lot of 'never' boxes, you could liken your approach to closing your eyes for 10 seconds while driving at speed on a motorway – not something I would ever recommend.

Anticipating resistance to change

Why do you resist change?

First, answer the questions yourself.

Then print out copies of the questionnaire and ask other members of the change planning team or leadership team to complete the questionnaire themselves, and compare results. Sharing it with others will give you a more measured response.

	HIGH	MEDIUM	LOW
Resistance to the desired state			
Can't envisage the desired state			
Would prefer a different solution			
Fear unknown outcomes			
Fear negative outcomes: loss of job/status/control/social structure			
Worry about the change being irreversible			
Feel that this change doesn't solve the problem			
Feel that I won't be able to learn the new way			
Can't see the relevance of the change to my work			
Resistance to going through the change state			
Don't know how to change			
Have other priorities occupying my energy			
Have experienced failed or painful change in the past			
Don't want a heavier workload			
Don't think the organisation can get through the transition			
Think that the change requires too much effort			

	HIGH	MEDIUM	LOW
Feel that I am too little involved			
Think that there are too many changes going on			
Resistance to leaving the current state			
Don't see the need to change			
Feel that the change is a criticism of performance			
Would rather focus on a different change			
Am too comfortable in the current state			
Value current skills above new ones			
Have a high sense of ownership of the way things work today			
Am reluctant to make any kind of change			
Do not believe management supports the need to make a change			

The questions in these checklists are aimed at raising awareness of what needs to be done to start to plan for new things, retain customers, be more profitable and outbox your competition. Remember, the more often the same reasons for resistance crop up, the higher the likelihood that you have accurately anticipated reasons for potential resistance.

 How can you use what you know about potential resistance to change in your organisation to create a plan to avoid these traps?

Action points

- Take time to research the big factors that create global change: especially the two biggest drivers of technology changes and population growth.

- Look more locally inside your own business, and pinpoint the real issues that mean you have no choice – you simply change or die.

- Use the PEST analysis to assess your own market changes.

- Complete the two downloadable audit tools that test how willing or able you are to start to make changes.

- Spend time with your colleagues to discuss all the factors that will lead to increased staff motivation and reduce resistance to change.

2

Why is change so hard?

Key points in this chapter:

- How to understand human psychology and responses, when it comes to working and changing.
- How you can gain powerful insights and ideas about how to lead people to change.
- How you can influence people by simply accommodating their thinking processes.
- How to accommodate some basic needs to speed up your change planning.

This book is not the place for an MA in psychology, but it is useful to have some idea about how people make decisions, how they compare themselves to others, and how they interact with their colleagues and their management team. As a manager who manages people, it is important that you know how people tick.

This knowledge will help you understand the key steps in the framework outlined later in the book. As I outline that framework, I will refer back to this section, because each and every step is based on how people work.

Core beliefs

They say that babies are born with only two fears: of falling and of loud noises. All their other fears and insecurities are what they learn, rehearse and create for themselves.

So you come into this world as a very simple little being, yet within just a handful of years you are the complex result of your environment, your parents, your friends, your experiences, mantras and rules from adults, and your own imagination. Every child is born roughly equal, yet within about five years the plan is set that will define your life and the way you will be.

Now it is always possible to change this plan, but few actually do. People somehow think that this is the way it is – this is who you are, these are your fears and understandings, your hopes and abilities.

You develop what are referred to as **core beliefs**, supported by 'evidence' that is sometimes just completely wrong. A dog barked at me once when I was small; he had sharp teeth and my mother told me it was dangerous. Cue the 'evidence' of an instruction from a trusted adult, the visual or imagined picture of the sharp teeth, and you have the ingredients for someone who is unlikely to work closely with dogs in the short term!

 What are your core beliefs? And what are the restrictive comments you may have stored away as 'evidence'?

Consider now this diversity of ability, thoughts, behaviours, phobias, beliefs and confidence (or lack of confidence), and think how it is present in the people that make up your organisation – oh, and don't forget, you are one of those people!

So now, going back to your basic issue of leading constant change, think how a request for change may be received by any one person.

Making decisions

In the 1960s a group of management scientists at the Stanford Research Institute (led by Robert F. Stewart, Albert Humphrey, Otis Benepe and Hal Eyring) were exploring how teams of people thought, operated and worked, and how the top team could be taught to plan out the future of the organisation. In particular, Otis Benepe looked at the process of decisions, which he saw as a **chain of logic**, as shown in Figure 2.1.

When confronted with a situation or an instruction that requires the person to act and change, their brain follows an appraisal process. There are three main steps.

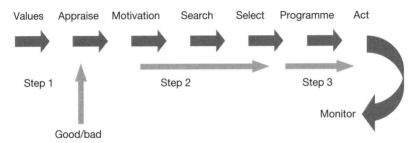

Figure 2.1 How people make decisions

1 First we make internal reference to our **values** and beliefs.
   If the individual is not comfortable with the change request,
   then progress stops and objections are returned in whatever
   form is decided – whether that is verbal, unspoken, inaction
   or walking away. If, however, we are able to accept that this is
   within our scope of values, then we move on to **appraise** the
   situation with whatever facts we have presented.

2 We then are governed by our **motivation** to proceed. This is
   the point where if we don't really want something, then our
   apathy will slow or even sabotage the process. The question
   everyone asks at this stage is 'What's in it for me?' Assuming
   we are motivated to continue, we then **search** for ranges of
   possible outcomes, and our creativity and knowledge will be
   the major factor here.

3 We then make a choice and **select** one of the courses of action
   or behaviour that we desire, forming a **programme** of action.
   We then **act** and deliver the outcome, and at the same time we
   monitor the responses we get and maybe accept feedback to
   modify the programme.

For most people, a simple decision cycle may take a few seconds, some
minutes at the most, and this process is going on all the time with all
your staff.

 How many decision cycles do you think are occurring at
any one point in time in your organisation?

MAKING DECISIONS WITHIN A TEAM

The process of managing constant change is a naturally occurring daily routine – made of up doing something, or finding something unexpected, or modifying what you do and then doing it all again. It is a constantly refining, moving feast that you consciously think about as little as the very act of breathing – fast, unconsciously driven and intuitive.

However, consider your organisation and the series of teams of people that operate within it. Figure 2.2 illustrates three sets of people, all with different backgrounds, ages, gender, ability and so on. The size of the arrows denotes positive movement (big arrows) or hesitancy and rejection towards a change programme. It shows how when people operate as a team then work slows down, changes are rejected or pushed into the long grass, and seemingly the team finds it difficult to agree to move forwards. In short, teams fail to perform.

 *Robert's Rules of Order*

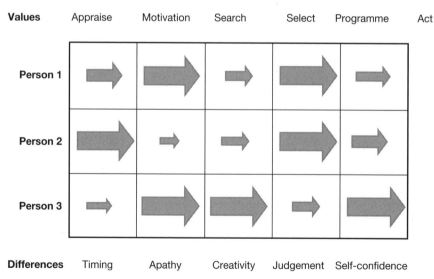

Values	Appraise	Motivation	Search	Select	Programme	Act
Person 1						
Person 2						
Person 3						
Differences	Timing	Apathy	Creativity	Judgement	Self-confidence	

Figure 2.2 Why teams fail to perform

Many meetings and discussions (especially in board rooms of most companies) follow **Robert's Rules of Order**, which were originally devised for the political environment. Its rules and etiquette encourage a civil, inclusive, non-confrontational method of running a team meeting, but they can also mean that many people with opinions are not given the chance to speak. So they can often block progress and mean that a meeting may never get to the 'truth' of the matter.

What's in it for me?

I have personally witnessed – and I am sure that you will have too – situations where value clashes have led to the total blockage of a change request. One of the main reasons why people resist change is because they ask themselves the question: 'What's in it for me?' Wherever you are in the organisation – from the CEO down to the most junior administrator – if you are truly honest with yourself, you will all ask yourself the same question.

In fact, according to the psychologists, you ask that question subconsciously 15 times a day. You are constantly assessing your environment, the relationships with your managers and colleagues, and the general perception of how the company is benefiting from your work, compared with what you get out of it.

> The American psychologist Frederick Herzberg identified a number of **hygiene factors**, which are basically the things that may not motivate you, but can demotivate you – like your working contract, pay, holiday, notice period etc. In contrast, **motivational factors** appeal to your need for personal growth. So money may be less important than recognition, responsibility, time with your manager, and opportunity for advancement.

To illustrate how people deal with daily change routines and pressures, Hal Eyring of the Stanford Research Institute team (mentioned earlier in this chapter) devised a model of **distributive justice**. I prefer to rename the model **personal justice**, since it relates to the person. It can be seen as a formula:

$$\frac{\text{Output}}{\text{Input (self)}} = \frac{\text{Output}}{\text{Input (company)}} = \text{Distributive justice (fairness)}$$

Inputs are what we put in:

- time
- qualifications
- experience
- loyalty
- discomfort
- personal skill
- connections
- creativity.

Outputs are what we get out:

- money
- satisfaction
- travel and time away
- perks
- training
- time with the boss
- recognition and advancement
- responsibility
- security.

To understand this model in context, you need to be aware of what happens when the model is not in balance. There are four phases to this imbalance, where the outputs and the inputs do not feel right:

1 **Re-perceive.** You try to justify the imbalance by explaining it in terms of temporary state, accepting the overriding need for it to be that way for a while, and acknowledging that there is a deserving reason for you to be more tolerant.

2 **Demand more**. You cannot re-perceive, or the time-based argument above has expired, leaving you feeling hard done by again. So you ask for more. It doesn't have to be money, but often starts off with that request. It is the feeling of being undervalued that you seek to correct.

3 **Give less**. The demanding more hasn't worked, and so you move to giving less, to balance the scales. You will notice when your own staff begin to give less – manifested in longer lunch breaks, time off sick and absenteeism, dentist appointments in the middle of a day, and a general slowing down. I suspect you've seen evidence of this in your own organisation – and now you know why.

4 **Attack**. All the attempts to reach a balance have failed, and so you resort to confrontation. This is not necessarily the physical type, but a formal process that may mean the individual leaves the employ of the business or ends up in a disciplinary process, or the company receives a formal grievance notice from the employee.

It is possible to move from balance to phase 3 and back again in the space of a few hours or days – this process is a constant ebb and flow and is often referred to as **engagement**.

Overcoming resistance

In my many years of working with executives and managers, I know that by this stage in any training programme they often have a despairing look on their faces! They, like you, may have recognised the symptoms and issues raised here and know just how difficult it is to move forward with teams of people.

But it is critical that you, as a leader, are able to identify the symptoms, understand the causes and plan to overcome any resistance to change.

Many CEOs and management teams have adopted a nickname for those who seek to block or resist change – they call them the **change saboteurs**. I have also met these change saboteurs myself, usually at the request of the executive teams, who see them to be blockages that cannot be tolerated and must be brought to task, or managed out of the organisation.

Invariably, when I speak with them, and ask them the right open questions, I receive a lucid and reasonable explanation for their perception of events and the issues they face. Often the blockage is simply hesitancy in the face of uncertainty, because they see reasons why the change will or may fail. The personal drivers holding them back are simply based on their differing understanding of the change request and how it sits with their own personal values and model of the world.

USING CONSISTENCY AND FAIRNESS

I am often asked, when advising clients on culture and change programmes:

- Does the style of the manager make any difference?
- Surely some people are better than others at leading change?
- Can great management be taught, or is it something that you've either got in your genes or not?

Interestingly, in the 1960s the Stanford Research Institute looked at styles such as:

- forces and threats
- persuasion (sales person techniques)
- incentive-based schemes (perks and rewards)
- participative/consultative approaches
- musical chairs (rotate, sack and replace).

The results suggested that style was not the dominating factor in determining the success of an individual in leading change. Instead, what was most important was a perception of **fairness** and **consistency**.

To the research teams of the day, this was confusing, since most work at that time used what is called a positivist approach – one that requires measurement and statistical understanding. The words 'perception' and 'fairness' were both subjective and contextual and incredibly difficult to model, measure and control. This was 'soft, fluffy' stuff, not the domain of mathematicians and scientists.

While 'consistency' is relatively quantifiable, 'fairness' is much more subjective. Yet it is one of the most popular words we use. Listen to politicians, who promise fair deals or a fair society. Listen to your children, who complain loudly when things are not fair.

So what exactly is fairness? You can look it up in the dictionary, which says: 'Treating people equally without favouritism or discrimination'. The problem is that we all have differing ideas, based upon our own backgrounds, values and beliefs, as to what constitutes favouritism and discrimination. It's a very subjective and contextual question.

Hal Eyring's distributive justice model shows how different people interpret the balance factors. So can you be fair to everyone in your workplace at the same time? The answer is obviously no!

However, because your organisation is not just a random selection of people dragged off the street, it seems that it can contain more similarities in values and beliefs than you might think. You tend to hire your people based on how they will 'fit in' – a common understanding of the world of your work and your organisation.

This is great news for managers, as it means you may be able to find some common ground of fairness after all. People are not so dogmatic that they say, 'It has to be completely fair, otherwise I resist'. They accept that some element of compromise is needed in life, and so they will accept fairness in sufficient measure to cross their 'acceptable-to-me' threshold.

You will know when you reach a person's threshold when they deem enough has been offered to make it sufficiently fair for them to accept. They will acknowledge this by using the words 'Fair enough'.

How often have you heard the phrase 'Fair enough' and not appreciated the compromise that has led to these words?

Fairness is thought to be the second most powerful driver for human emotive response, beating most of the seven deadly sins, such as greed, envy and gluttony (but falling into second place behind the 'promise of sex' as the most powerful driver for human emotive response!).

Fairness is also perhaps the most powerful driver in a professional sense. But if fairness is a perception, then just how do we get it and how do we make life fair for our teams in order to gain a positive response? In Chapter 4 I will tell you how to engage your workforce and teams in the fairest way yet conceived, by asking them just one question.

AVOIDING RISK

Another reason why change is hard is because of the issues of risk and trust.

There are many reasons why you might avoid risk.

- The idea of changing something takes you right back to your childhood conditioning, which usually associates change with risk. This risk is usually associated with your discomfort on a personal level, but you have human instincts that take you to a safe place automatically.
- In your business training – whether in finance, a process situation, manufacturing, or a repeating service – you are taught to reduce variation in outcomes and to standardise processes. By reducing risks and mistakes, you therefore reduce your costs. You are often rewarded for taking variation out of a situation, and for making the outcome totally predictable. Then you measure it to death, and produce pretty reports and graphs to show how well it has been done.

- You may also have a personal fear associated with change and its possible outcomes. Because you are moving away from the known and tested methods, there is a chance and a definite risk that change may cause failure and expose you to your critics, with possible ramifications.

And so you are taught throughout your childhood and into your early business training that risk is something to be avoided – to be planned out of the equation. Unfortunately the word 'risk' becomes inextricably linked with the word 'change'.

 What events from your own life might have led you to avoid risks?

Change thinking

So there are a number of reasons why change can be so hard.

- People are all different – with varying backgrounds, beliefs and values.
- Just because they wear work clothes does not mean they have abandoned the child within.
- Teams and team working using Robert's Rules of Order can slow down or even stop progress.

As a leader, you need to be able to rise above the noise of psychological resistance and try to create an environment of **change thinking**. When organisations have this approach, it is often much easier to 'unstick' people from the old ways, and move them to a new place that serves both themselves and the business in the future.

There are many reasons why it is so difficult to break out of an existing way of thinking.

- The old world **looks successful**, even though its time has passed and change is needed.
- Those involved with the new world have little or no **proven history** they can point to.

- The new world has no trusted or recognised **language** to link it to your people.
- The old world has so much invested in it, it is difficult to **justify** making the change.
- The timing of change usually means it occurs while the old world is still considered **fit for purpose**.
- People resist change because change **hurts**, or so they believe.

 *Change thinking*

Do you welcome change?

The following questions ask you to score your approach to various actions and activities that provide a change-thinking environment. Print out the questionnaire and see if the answers you scored yourself are shared by others in your organisation. This could be an audit for starting a new approach to change thinking, with anonymous input from your teams.

	NEVER	HARDLY	SOMETIMES	MOSTLY	ALWAYS
Your organisation reviews staff regularly					
You celebrate good ideas or innovation					
Everyone in the organisation has a voice					
You send your teams to learn or experience something new every month					
You can point to a monthly learning experience for yourself					
You are excited about work and show it					
You measure change formally and report it separately to the daily work					

	NEVER	HARDLY	SOMETIMES	MOSTLY	ALWAYS
You communicate the organisation's mission, vision and objectives each quarter					
You recognise attempts to change something, even when it fails					
HR manages difficult situations with your direct reports					
You are always available to your colleagues, peers, teams and superiors					
You are comfortable with public speaking within your organisation					
You have a culture of learning and exploring new ideas					
You invite suppliers to pitch new products regularly					
You circulate learning material or good articles to your teams					
People suggesting change are welcomed with open arms					
Challenges are seen as an opportunity to change things for the better					
Even the quiet people have a chance to say something in meetings					

HOW ORGANISATIONS REALLY WORK

The research of the Stanford Research Institute in the 1960s included seven key findings that were so controversial they were never published. The insight they give will help you weave the framework for change into your own business.

 *The seven key findings*

- A business can be divided into two parts: the base business plus the development business. The development business turns over every five to seven years. (This was a major surprise because it emphasised the need for a better method for planning and managing change.)
- All people measure what they get from their work and divide it by what they give to the work. This reward/effort ratio is then compared with others. If it is perceived as too low, the person slows down.
- The introduction of a corporate planner, or centralised planning team, upsets the sense of fair play at a senior level, making the job of the corporate planner impossible.
- The gap between what could be done by the organisation and what is actually done is about 35 per cent.
- The senior person will over-supervise the area they come from.
- There are three factors that separate excellence from mediocrity:
  - overt attention to purchasing and resourcing
  - written departmental plans for short-term improvement
  - continued education of the senior executives.
- Formal documentation is required for approval of development work. In short, it is not possible to solve the problem by stopping planning.

Remember that these findings were never published at the time of writing, because of the far-reaching consequences of adopting these principles. We will return to them later in this book.

Why then is change so hard?

Going back to the question posed by this chapter – why is change so hard?

- People instinctively resist change, preferring the here and now.
- People fear change, due to their background, experiences and attitudes.

- People always ask the question, 'What's in it for me?'
- There has to be a 'pay back' for making change.
- Fairness is a huge driver for a happy outcome.
- Communication is critical during periods of change.
- Your own management style is not a factor in your success, as long as you are consistent and fair.
- People gather as a herd at times of change, so knowing how they operate is an advantage to dealing with their resistance.
- People are creatures of habit – your job is to make your change their new habit.

Action points

- Think about the basic human responses that will block or prevent your change plan from working.
- Take some time to identify the big question: 'What's in it for me?' The distributive justice model explains a lot of people's behaviour and reluctance to change, and what may be happening right now in your organisation.
- Use fairness as one of the most powerful platforms for getting your change plan to work.
- Decide the steps that you will take to create a culture of change thinking in your business – because it is change thinking that will 'unstick' people and allow them to change and move forwards.
- Remember that people instinctively resist change – your role is to help them overcome this, and to change willingly.

3

What are the secret ingredients of effective change?

Key points in this chapter:

- How to install trust and fairness as a background to increased performance.
- How to engage your staff properly.
- How to set your strategic direction.
- Why you need to understand the money.
- How to fix the management biases.

By the end of this chapter you will have prepared your organisation for the 15-step framework for leading constant change. As any good chef will tell you, the trick to a really great plate of food is to start with the right ingredients. So first you need to be aware of the concepts behind the framework.

 **The Holy GRAIL**

Any change framework needs to follow certain principles, which can be easily remembered by the acronym **GRAIL** – this is the Holy GRAIL of leading constant change.

- **Governance**. The framework must be robust and contained as a transferable skill.
- **Repeatable**. It needs to allow for constant change, which happens all the time.
- **Auditable**. It must be possible to measure real financial results.
- **Inclusive**. The change must involve all stakeholders.
- **Led strategy**. The change should be led by the organisation's leader and not operationally driven; companies that plan

strategically will succeed over those that simply manage operationally.

How to install trust and fairness

Two of the key ingredients in any people management situation, but especially one involving change, are trust and fairness.

Fair play is vital in the organisation in order to motivate and commit people to a change project. Remember, 'What's in it for me?' is the single most repeated (often unspoken) question of all.

Fair play has to do with the expectations that people have towards justice being met – it is about what is 'just' treatment and how this is being distributed inside the organisation. In other words, it is the expectations that individual employees have about what they will receive (personal outputs) for the work they are doing (personal inputs), compared with what others receive or give.

All too easily, a company can find itself in a situation with low morale, poor performance, people not taking initiative or simply passing the blame for low yields, instead of enjoying the planned-for benefits intended by the management.

In contrast, a sense of fair play has many benefits for the company:

- It increases the motivation of employees because they feel more secure and have positive attitudes about their jobs.
- It makes employees more open to new things because they have lost their fear of involvement – because they trust that management's intentions are good.

So how do you create the perception of fair play in your business?

In any collective system, such as a work organisation, the set of expectations and learned behaviours is referred to as the organisational **memes**. More commonly known as 'the way we do things around here', the memes are the thoughts and ways of interacting that are learned and adopted, and also shared and replicated. They are often passed on with great care and detail to newcomers, to ensure their continued adoption.

 What are the memes that are passed on in your own organisation when a new person arrives?

In practice you can see this clearly when new ideas or new supervisors and managers are introduced at all levels of the business. For example, when a new manager arrives, they are looked upon as someone who may upset the rules of the game – demanding that people work harder, without extra compensation, and then taking the credit for the work as if it was their own. Suspicion is rife until shown to be otherwise. As a consequence, the more the manager insists on doing something new, the worse the situation becomes. The manager cannot win.

So what can you do about it? Hal Eyring suggested that, when introducing a new idea or a new manager to the organisation, the company should:

- understand the way the change will affect individuals;
- find out the personal value system that influences the conduct of the individuals working in the organisation – what each person considers to be a reasonable input and what outcome (compensation) is considered fair;
- make sure that every new idea, system or person will provide a net profit to the plans that are already in the company.

To make a change more acceptable, the best way is to establish the concept of fair play even before the change is being introduced. You do this by communicating what the desired result will be and how it will affect the overall company situation – in other words, answer the question, 'What's in it for everyone?'

This is because the perception of justice works at both an individual and a group level. Unfortunately there are all too many examples of companies failing to implement their change programmes because they have not given any thought to what is really in it for the employees.

Case study
Fair play

The perception of fairness can affect the earnings potential of a company, as in the case of Wensum Clothing Company. Through a developmental change planning session held in 1997, they uncovered 600 issues (received anonymously from all staff), of which 35 per cent had to do with the unfairness of the bonus system. Teams were getting penalised for poor production that was caused by absence of material to work with, rather than their lack of skills, or attitudes, or lower personal productivity. The material problem was put right and the bonus element of the system was reduced from 60 per cent to 25 per cent – and the production went up from 1,100 to 1,700 units per week.

So the cultural backdrop to any and every change management approach must be the idea of establishing fairness in everything you do. And to make any change truly successful, it must be led by those at the head of the organisation, but be acceptable to those at the point of impact.

As well as the need to create fairness, the other key ingredients in an effective change management framework may be summarised in four main performance concepts:

- participative planning
- strategic appraisal
- financial understanding
- unbiased teams.

Together, these concepts underpin the framework set out in this book for leading constant change.

Participative planning

Involvement is a key concept in leading change. Any change programme needs the participation of everyone in the company – from the security guard at the gate to the chairman or owner of the company. Everyone needs to be involved in planning what requires to be done for the successful development of a business.

Participative planning is the system that creates motivation and commitment to the project. It is an approach that has two main purposes:

- to involve all participants
- to provide a framework for trust and fair play.

Participative planning makes annual plans and budgets much easier and more effective by gathering ideas and information from all participants, and then turning them into action plans created for and by the participants.

A key factor is that when employees are asked for their ideas they should be asked to write on a simple and **anonymous form**, if possible with a cost and/or benefit statement (although in the vast majority of cases employees may not feel they have the skills to do this). By inviting comments in this way, ideas flow in – though often of vastly mixed quality.

It is the job of the appointed **change planning team** or committee to sift through these inputs – which might range from 'Why don't we oil the canteen doors?' to 'Why don't we open a company in Japan?'. The disparity of these hypothetical examples is deliberate – they might look absurd on paper, but in practice the system works. The canteen doors get oiled, if that is what is needed to increase the quality of work, and the employees get to understand why it is not possible to open up a company in Japan (or, perhaps, the senior management begin to think about the advantages of opening a company in Japan).

Case study
Ideas gathering

At Bemrose, a medium-sized printing and packaging corporation in the UK, a member of the transport department asked why the company used hired transport to deliver to its French customers. Would it not be cheaper and better to use its own vehicles? The idea was made part of an action programme by the change planning team, and a person was designated to investigate the problem and its costs, with a time period specified in which to implement action. In this case it was discovered that it was cheaper and better to use the company's own transport for the French deliveries, and so that practice was adopted.

The result was not only more efficiency (because it was cheaper), but also a better image for the company and vastly improved morale among the employees, who had made a real difference to management decision making. Management, too, were grateful – after all, they knew they could not think of everything, so were happy to take on board other people's ideas.

Participative planning also provides a framework for trust and fair play, which automatically has a positive influence on work motivation. This is because participative planning is a way of breaking down the barriers that exist between the board, executive management and the workforce. The idea is to dignify the individual in the job they are doing and allow their views to be heard in a constructive way, while at the same time preserving the authority structure.

 Form1 Planning issue

In the change framework outlined in this book, employees and stakeholders can tell senior management about any criticisms or

Team Action Management

Delivers successful change and increased performance
to all people based organisations

Form 1: Your views/opinions

Please give a short title _____ *Cheaper distribution* _____

Decide which box your title refers to and tick only 1

PRESENT	OR	FUTURE	
Strength ☐		Opportunity ☐
Fault ✓		Threat ☐

· Statement of your view or opinion – 1 per form please

*Would it not be cheaper and better to do it
in our own vehicles?*

· Do you want to give an example?

*We could save money by not outsourcing to
foreign transport companies*

· What could be done

*Look at the costs and see if this is better
for the company*

Unleashing the power

TAM Uk Plc © 2008 Team Action Management ™

Figure 3.1 Sample Form1 (planning issue)

suggestions by submitting (anonymously) a provisional **planning issue** (using Form1). This is designed to allow each person to express their feelings about how the business is being run, or specifically comment on a proposed change plan or ideas for change.

Step 4 (in Part 2) describes in detail how this form is filled in, but an example of a Form1 submission, from an anonymous employee, is shown in Figure 3.1.

This pool of ideas is then transferred to the action planning group, and is an indication of how people want to participate and how they trust the management to listen to their suggestions.

The advantage of using this anonymous form is that it makes it possible to gather ideas from right across the organisation. In most organisations, it is not possible to ask everyone what their thoughts or views are at the same time. Imagine gathering all your staff into one great big room and asking them what they think – the result would either be absolute quiet, a roar of noise as they offered you big ideas or opinions, or more likely a noise of conversation, as they discuss things among themselves rather than with you (because it's safer that way).

In most organisations where a structure of management exists, highlighting an issue at the 'lower level' in the organisation often leads to it being subject to open scrutiny by the various supervisory and management layers. Very soon the idea will be knocked over by various preconceptions as to why it couldn't happen, or dismissed because it would upset the status quo, or stolen by a person who has reason to portray the idea as their own.

In contrast, the anonymous engagement method allows a simultaneous 'conversation' to take place with every employee and stakeholder, with no threat to any individual. It releases the potential of everyone in the company – from the chairman to the unskilled worker.

More importantly, the work of the change planning team is subject to transparency and audit, so it considers the undiluted input of everyone involved – there is no possibility for individuals to remove, generalise or delete the ideas offered.

CEOs of larger companies often voice a common complaint: 'My management team feeds me bullshit'. What they mean is that almost

Case study
Filtering out the truth

Some years ago a well-known camera film manufacturer set out to make a super-fast film for the professional industry. It was a deviation from the company's normal products and had never been done before.

The CEO took an active interest, as it represented a large opportunity in the market. He attended the laboratory regularly to oversee progress. Week after week went by, with variations to chemicals, temperature and substrate being monitored and tested. Each week the tests failed. At the end of nearly 20 weeks of trialling and exploring, the results were negative. The conclusion of the technical director was that this was an aspirational programme but not physically possible to achieve, so he ordered the cessation of the project.

As the instruction to stop was given, the CEO happened by. He stopped and chatted to the technician responsible for setting up the various tests and lamented the fact that the product was impossible. The technician responded by telling the CEO that it was in fact possible and he knew how to do it. The CEO ordered him to proceed and the technician brought together a combination of substrate material, chemicals and temperature control that had not yet been tried. The result – it worked! The CEO angrily asked the technician why he had stood by and watched the company waste large amounts of time and money to test failed combinations. The technician's response? 'It wasn't my place – nobody asked me.'

every piece of information that they receive has been created or edited by a professional manager, who has applied the 'CEO filter' to the process.

All too often CEOs receive sanitised reports that show how well things are being managed, until such a time when they become unmanageable. Only then does the CEO get the undiluted real version.

So the adage that it's a lonely job at the top becomes reality.

Often companies hire brilliant people, but even if the people are not all brilliant they can be great at what they do. Just because they operate within a managed structure of reporting, with job descriptions and reviews, does not mean that they are not able to think, innovate and act in good faith for the whole business, rather than only their small part of it.

Case study
Using staff talent

I recently spoke with a man approaching retirement, who told me that in the large warehouse for which he and a colleague were responsible they had written a little piece of software that automated batch entry of data during the booking-in process. He told me that to do it the 'company way' took about 4 hours per day, yet with their little program it took 20 seconds, allowing them to run the warehouse more efficiently and with fewer staff members.

Another manufacturing company had accounting issues in the way it counted and recorded stock figures. By engaging the Form1 process above, it discovered that a lathe operator had an MBA in computer science and could fix a problem that would otherwise cost thousands of pounds in external help. He was able to offer help through the Form1 model, whereas his idea had previously been rejected by the operations manager, because it would have taken him away from the lathe operations for a while.

What examples of this type of worker participation can you recall from your own experience?

STAFF ENGAGEMENT

When you think about worker participation, it is important to consider **staff engagement** generally. Of course, you have already 'engaged' the services of your staff by way of an employment contract. But staff can be very variable in their work ethic, habits, positive attitude, and willingness to produce work with sufficient effort.

A whole management science has built up around the concept of engagement and there are many theories as to how you can maximise the effort of each person you employ. Shocking statistics suggest that only 26 per cent of your staff are fully engaged; that is, happily working very hard almost all the time, and actively interested in their work, their teams and the business itself. About 60 per cent of your people are in the middle category: turning up for work and doing the minimum that is necessary to maintain their jobs. They move up and down the distributive justice model (see Chapter 2) and produce only around 55 per cent of their potential work.

The big shocker is the rest: the 14 per cent or so who are what is described as 'disengaged'. Often this is not enough to lead to any disciplinary action, but these people are known to be 'difficult', 'confrontational', or 'blockers'. Nobody seems to know how to manage them, and so they carry on.

These people are turning up to work and being paid each day. But they have mentally quit. The most difficult group to engage with are in this 'quit but stayed' category.

I have watched with fascination the farcical attempts that organisations have made to improve engagement. The list of methods is long and painful, but here are a few, with the reasons why they usually fail.

- **The survey**. This is a real favourite – the litmus test of how much engagement apparently exists in your company. A number of specially devised questions are sent around to all staff, with the request that they submit their answers for analysis. The questions include how they feel about themselves, their colleagues, their managers and the company itself. Some of these surveys are anonymous, and some ask good questions. However, there are many problems with written surveys.

- The questions asked may not be the questions that the respondent wants to answer.
- The range of possible answers may not include the one the respondent wants to submit.
- The questions mean something different to each person, depending on their role within the business.
- The answers may be contextual, but provide no means for saying so.
- The anonymity is not clear, and by disclosing gender, age group and main focus, the respondent may well give up their anonymity.
- The act of asking may itself provide a result that is not scientific or balanced.
- The survey may provide an opportunity for the protest of non-return.
- The survey may also allow an individual to stir things up (because they can) and for the hostile respondent to vent their anger in the knowledge that they cannot be discovered.

- **Focus groups**. These ask a group or groups of representative workers to take time out of their day job and attend a structured meeting to consult on subjects or issues (the same approach is used on 'away days', or any activity specifically designed to get people to open up). This feedback is then gathered into a report and presented as a fact. Issues here include:
  - Lack of anonymity and the fact that in a group people may feel threatened by the repercussions – real or imagined – to the feedback they provide. So they tell it how it needs to be represented, not as reality or truth.

- The selection process of who should attend the meeting is often faulty, as quieter, more reserved people may not wish to expose themselves to the process, even though they may have great ideas. In contrast, the louder, more forceful individuals, who are able to voice opinions successfully, are happy to be chosen. So the focus group is not a fair representation of a team or department.
- There are also problems with the structure of these meetings: the bias in the agenda and the loaded questions. Peers are often cautious about responding truthfully or completely in such an environment, and so this approach is rarely successful.

- **The newsletter**. This should not to be confused with 'communication', as it is only one way the company may try to get a message across. Unfortunately, it should also not be confused with engagement, as it is a very blunt instrument for informing people about a situation or issue, with no feedback mechanism.

- **Extra information**. I've watched companies try to provide transparency in numbers, processes and decisions. In some cases this does encourage increased interest, but in others it simply provides reasons for more problems or invites more criticism.

- **Performance rewards**. These may often be confused with engagement, thanks to the look of delight on the faces of those who get a financial bonus. But this delight may last for a very short time, and then be forgotten, or the financial reward may be accepted but then criticised for being too small. The best performance rewards are non-financial and are personally adapted to suit the individual. The best award I ever gave an employee was one he chose: a karaoke machine worth £700, which he received as a bonus for substantial sales over-performance. It met his personal needs and aspirations and was a motivator for a long time – despite his wife's despair when he took it home!

So there are many ways in which organisations attempt to engage with staff. Most of them are very short-lived experiences and most fail – not because of the lack of good intent from the company, but because they do not have a true purpose or an action-based outcome.

 What are the main methods you use in your organisation to engage staff? How successful are they?

For true engagement to take place, there needs to be an answer to the question 'What's in it for me?' – or, better still, 'What's in it for us?' The only way to do this is to link engagement with action and outcome: **active engagement**.

Participative planning, involving all staff – simultaneously and anonymously through the system of the Form1 – provides the richest and deepest audit of the company that you will ever have the pleasure of doing. This is because it:

- seeks an opinion on a question set by the business leader – and therefore has a **purpose**;
- sends a message of **active inclusion** (unlike most other engagement methods);
- **gathers data** and information that has not been seen before;
- **excites** the organisation around the common challenges of the organisation's future;
- is **action**-orientated, because all staff know that there will be some follow-on activity;
- provides a **unified vision** for establishing changes and forward planning.

Strategic appraisal

Another main component in leading constant change is strategic appraisal:

- How do the intended changes affect the company's strategic objectives?

- Do the actions of the change project contribute in a positive way to give the company better results, more sales, more profits, or higher customer satisfaction?

'Managing change' is in fact **project management**. And project management is like the single cell structure that builds into any form of forward-looking management system, including corporate planning, long-range or strategic planning, business planning, managing by objectives, or simple budgeting.

To plan in a strategic sense, you need to return to the market and the environment audits (Chapter 1), so that you can see the bigger picture that allows you to set a strategic course for the business. A statement of strategy can then set out – in broad terms – the considerations and plans that will allow the organisation to navigate through the complex and often changing external environment.

If you have no strategy, it is like being without a map to show you where to start from and where you intend to end up.

So it is important not to try to lead change simply from an operational point of view. To do so is to ignore the external factors and pressures that the business will face along the way, and will make the business vulnerable to forced and unexpected changes from others. What is more, if there is no real defined impact on the business, then the change project will inevitably lose support from within and will eventually fail to deliver meaningful results.

In many TQM (Total Quality Management) projects, for example, changes and improvements have often seemed to take first priority – change for change's sake – without being directed at achieving actual results for the company. The problem is that actions for improvement are not aligned with the overall strategic plan of the company, so they may provide direction or results that are not wanted or needed by the company's business plan.

Sometimes a change programme is focused on a desired strategic objective in a far-off and un-committing future, and then people will have difficulties visualising that future. It is therefore necessary to refocus on what will increase productivity today, as well as what will develop the business tomorrow.

So a change programme needs to be linked with the operational day-to-day business of the company, always making sure it provides positive results for the company and strengthens the company's strategies.

The challenge is to balance short-term gains with longer-term objectives. If people do not see any real results coming from their hard work, they will quickly lose their inspiration and the change programme will experience a major setback. Unfortunately many managers pay less attention to strategy and prefer to look after their own day-to-day fire-fighting efforts, instead of adhering to pre-established plans. It is after all what they get measured and paid on, isn't it?

LEADING CHANGE

In my experience, if a company wants to make sure the strategic plans are put in practice, then it needs to involve more people than just the top management or a strategic planner when making those plans. Because although the executives may dictate the direction of the long-term strategic plans, those plans can only be implemented successfully if there is participation from all the people with responsibility in key areas. So the people who are going to work on a specific project or be involved in the normal day-to-day running of the company should be directly involved in what is to be done.

In this way, an understanding of where the company is going will lead to more commitment to the execution of the plans (which the staff themselves have had a part in making). There is also less fear about management's intentions and instead a sense of fair play, because all the employees have participated in the company's decision-making process.

However, this process still needs a team leader who is disciplined and is prepared to police the actions of those involved, according to a pre-established agenda and through the monitoring phase of the implementation. The control of the planning must remain in the hands of management, even though there is a high degree of worker participation. One way to do this is to make sure that the involvement and decisions of the workers are always supported by the manager responsible for that particular area, and approved by a higher authority before being implemented.

Even though the change planning framework involves all staff, management should not lose the control of the decisions or outcome activity. So while the change planning sessions use input from all levels of the company hierarchy, it is the change planning team that decides what strategic actions will lead to the desired longer-term objectives set by the company.

BUSINESS FILTER

For a business to operate successfully, it needs to develop strategic plans in six interrelated areas. These are the areas that give the company its *raison d'être*, and therefore all improvement plans must be assessed by a short/medium and long-term strategic evaluation in each of these areas. (Later chapters refer to these areas as the **business filter**.) The six areas are:

- **Product/service**. What it is and how it works, and when and where to make improvements.
- **Process**. How it will be made and/or assembled, subcontracting and purchasing, and labour and machinery.
- **Customers**. Who will buy it and how they can be persuaded to purchase the product.
- **Distribution**. How the product/service will be stored, transported and delivered.
- **Finance**. Where the money will come from and how the cash flow will be controlled.
- **Administration**. How the company will be managed, the management style, the organisation structure and the people-skills needed.

To cover all these areas, any development project will therefore need six quite different sets of skills, abilities and personalities. These must be brought together and welded into a formal programme for the project to succeed. Ideally, the strategic thinking should not be outsourced, since a company will benefit greatly if they can develop a core competence in strategic thinking among executives from all areas of the business.

At the same time, it is also important that the programme is not rigid. It needs the flexibility to change direction when signals – from any area of the business – are raised.

Case study
Strategic planning

Peter Bennett, former chief executive of the British newsagent group WHSmith, introduced a change framework into the group in the 1970s, setting the base for the group's strategic planning and control activities. Each element of the plan – usually production, marketing, finance, administration and new projects – was given to a study group, which made proposals for implementing it (the action programme). If top managers asked for modifications to the plans that hit their desks, their requests were the subject of additional study. Within weeks or months the groups had reported, the budget and long-term plans were modified, and the orders were sent out to implement the recommendations of the study groups.

Every November, senior managers in the various divisions gathered for a five-day session to draw up plans for the next five years. But now they were no longer working without a guide. Since the system generated a five-year plan, all that had to be done was to 'recycle' year two of the previous year's budget and tack an additional year on to the end.

Financial understanding

- Do you reach your long-term company objectives (usually ROI or ROCE) through your everyday actions?
- Does everyone with any responsibility in the company know the financial consequences of what they are doing?

Understanding 'why' we do the things that we do affects the way people work. If the improvement objectives have not had the desired effect on the business result, you might have to change the way you work – maybe several times within short intervals. This can be especially frustrating for employees, who may be told to do things differently perhaps for the third time around. But if everybody learns how their actions contribute to the numbers then it is easier to make people understand why they have to change.

Why learn finance? Basically because, in a commercial organisation, finance is the bottom line of the business. Everything that is being done links up to the financial results of the company. So when making an action programme, one of the first steps is to evaluate the current position of the company and translate this information into functional cost and sales statements.

First, projections should be made on 'What if?' situations and the results calculated. Later, when the final action programme is to be decided, a formal profit and loss statement and a balance sheet must be prepared, which forecast the cash flow of the operation and explain the specific actions that will lead to the success of the development or change project.

Financial training does not need to be particularly ambitious, but it is essential that every responsible person working on any development or change project has an understanding of the financial implications of the work projected – both for budgeting and monitoring purposes.

- Have your directors attended a finance course, and can they read a balance sheet?
- Has your senior management team attended a finance course and can they read a profit and loss document and understand cash flows?
- Have your key workers (who order goods or materials, or make purchases and organise resources) been on a finance course to understand budgets and cash flow implications?

Simple concepts, such as the difference between 30-day credit terms and 30-day net credit terms, can affect your company's cash flow by up to 30 days – either in your favour, or against you. The question relates to timing of invoices, much of which depends on the timing of decisions taken at a lower level in your organisation. So it is important that there is an understanding of finance at every level in the organisation.

Without training and understanding, you allow your company to operate without controls.

Unbiased teams

Unbiased teams are a way of organising group work. Most project teams fail to reach common ground on what actions to take because of internal politics or problems with cohesive organisation cultures. The same people in a work group or a project team may be successful or not, depending on the way the group process is structured.

Not reaching an agreement because of conflict between different departments or between persons usually ends up with a senior person deciding on what to do, without reaching a consensus or commitment on the part of the participants. It is as destructive as the decision-making situations where there is a 'hearing' of opinions from the people concerned, before the executive decides on what is to be done. There is little effective participation and the advantages that can be gained from good team work have been lost.

The situation becomes worse when the group reaches agreement on the basis of consensus and conformity. This phenomenon is a result of **groupthink**: members of the group try not to be too harsh in their judgements of their leader or their colleagues. Instead, they adopt a soft line of criticism, even in their own thinking. So in meetings all members are amiable and seek complete concurrence on every important issue, with no bickering or conflict to spoil the cosy, 'we' atmosphere. Again, the formality of Robert's Rules of Order may apply and can significantly dilute the outcome of the process.

> The concept of **groupthink** was outlined first by the psychologist Irvin Janis in 1972 (*Victims of Groupthink: a Psychological Study of Foreign-Policy Decisions and Fiascoes*, Houghton Mifflin). His influential work was taken up and refined by later studies.

In a cohesive group, the danger is not that each individual will fail to reveal their objections to another person's proposal, but that they will think the proposal is a good one, without making a careful, critical scrutiny of the pros and cons of the alternatives. The more cohesive the group, the greater the inner compulsion on the part of each member to avoid disunity, which encourages them to believe in the soundness of whatever proposals are promoted by the leader or by a majority of the group's members.

There are many undesired consequences of groupthink. The group:

- limits its discussions to a few alternative courses of action (often only two), without an initial survey of any better alternatives;
- fails to re-examine the course of action initially preferred by the majority, even when it learns of risks and drawbacks it had not originally considered;
- spends little or no time discussing whether there are overlooked non-obvious gains, or ways of reducing the seemingly prohibitive costs in the rejected alternatives;

- makes little or no attempt to obtain information from experts within its own organisation, who might be able to supply more precise estimates of potential losses and gains;
- shows positive interest in facts and opinions that support its preferred policy, but tends to ignore facts and opinions that do not;
- spends little time considering how the chosen policy might be hindered by bureaucratic inertia, sabotaged by political opponents, or temporarily derailed by common accidents; consequently, it fails to work out contingency plans to cope with foreseeable setbacks that could endanger the overall success of its chosen course.

 Do you recognise the symptoms of groupthink in your company? Does groupthink exist to the detriment of the effectiveness of your senior leadership teams?

The framework of this book deliberately avoids groupthink, because it creates a set of rules of behaviour in the teamwork sessions. I believe that you actually want to have some conflict and criticism flowing in a controlled manner, and the key to this is **unbiased teams**.

These syndicate teams, of two or three members of the project team, are allocated items from the change planning issues that are *not related* to their usual sphere of responsibility. For example, the accountant may be given suggestions concerned with sales and marketing.

This is done in order to:

- familiarise each planner with areas of business for which they have no day-to-day accountability;
- ensure that issues are examined without the preconceptions inevitably held by experts in that particular area.

Tentative action plans are then subjected to group discussion, where the responsible person from each area has the chance to comment on why one proposal is or is not viable to the project. The 'controlled conflict' that this debate creates helps the team members to clear up many misunderstandings and misconceptions about what other departments are doing in the company.

This approach may at first sound counterintuitive, but it allows participants who would normally not cooperate to commit themselves to some of the proposed plans for their area, because they see that other departments are committing themselves to something that they themselves have already suggested earlier in another syndicate.

Another clear advantage of using this way of working is that the managers who participate in the planning sessions can influence the embryo plans of their colleagues in other disciplines. Everybody will then work towards the same goals, having found a common ground with the other departments.

The possibility of achieving things that were unthinkable before is now real, because the participants can forget about existing stereotypes and personal differences, thus breaking down interdepartmental and professional barriers. And in the end each participant will have an action plan for their own department that is interlinked with the other department plans; all agreed upon and committed to by everyone in the presence of everyone. At the very least, those whose operations are likely to be affected by the plans of another department are forewarned of what is in store for them.

Case study
Using unbiased teams

In one non-profit research institute the director was faced with over a hundred members of staff with PhDs, who considered themselves superior and above the profit motive. They believed in science for science's sake, and the privilege to work as they wished. The problem was that the profit motive was not understood and so there was little collaboration with non-research management. The institute was losing money and was fast becoming a major embarrassment to the City and the 23 universities that supported its operations. Using unbiased teams helped to get rid of professional jealousy and the superiority complex that was damaging relationships between the scientists and the non-research management.

Another example is the case of a large printing and publishing company. Although publicly traded, it still retained a lingering paternalism that stemmed from its earlier 'family company' status. The chief executive, who replaced the retiring family chairman, promoted a young sales and marketing manager over the heads of six older managing directors of smaller subsidiaries and major sub-groups, making him the new group managing director. Not surprisingly, this resulted in considerable discontent and led to lack of cooperation, with each executive keeping his own subsidiary tightly within his own control. Management politics and the perceived unfairness created by the promotion began to split up the company. By introducing unbiased teams, it was possible to create greater harmony and nurture a 'group spirit', without changing the personalities.

How the performance concepts work together

This chapter has outlined the four performance concepts that are necessary for a successful framework for leading constant change. The common thread between them, of course, is that it is your people who drive your organisation.

- **Participative planning** looks at how you can engage your people in a fair and systematised way, allowing them the dignity of involvement at the point of change.

- **Strategic appraisal** stresses the importance of linking change to strategy – otherwise what is change, apart from fiddling while Rome burns? People need to understand the results of their hard work.

- **Financial understanding** forces you – and your team – to confront the money. Although profit is not the only driver, budgets and cash flow are common to most businesses, and poor cash flow and lack of understanding of finance lead to more failures than anything else.
- **Unbiased teams** avoid protectionism in your departments. By using unbiased teams you are able to gain greater understanding, more interdepartmental acceptance and can start to manage your business holistically rather than in silos.

The key responsibility of top-level executives is the successful management of constant change. And it is these performance concepts that will provide the basis for an effective change management framework.

Action points

- Plan how to install trust and fairness as a background to ensure you get the performance you want.
- Discuss with your human resources team the best ways to engage your staff.
- Set out your strategic direction in writing.
- Take training if you are not sure that you understand the money.
- Think about how you can fix the management biases.

4

How do I use and install a change framework?

Key points in this chapter:

- Why you need to use a defined framework.
- How to design the framework.
- How the framework works.
- How to install the framework in your business.

Why do you need a framework for leading constant change? Understanding and adopting a framework will give you:

- a deeper understanding of the change issues;
- a greater internal resource and capability;
- a solid cultural shift to improve fairness and trust;
- a worker engagement method that has respect;
- greater control of your business;
- improved performance, which delivers increased profit or customer satisfaction;
- a flexibility that can outperform competitors and adapt to shifts in the market or business model.

Figure 4.1 illustrates how this framework works.

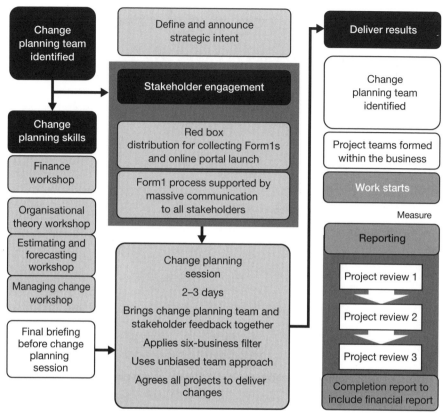

Figure 4.1 The framework for leading constant change

The framework for leading constant change

This framework can be implemented as a six-week, repeatable programme, via knowledge transfer to your senior team, but it requires just six days of their time. It simultaneously engages all your stakeholders and staff, but takes up just 10 minutes of their precious time, and provides the cultural platform on which to output the developmental and corrective work required to achieve results.

 *Framework schematic*

The framework is a fully integrated management system, which will accelerate company development in a controlled manner.

The key to using the framework successfully is that everybody is involved in writing the business operating and change plan, and employees from all levels are asked to set targets and suggest ideas for lifting the company's performance. In addition, they are encouraged to learn about areas outside their own specialities, to give them an overall understanding of the rationale behind decisions that will affect them.

So the attributes of a framework for successfully leading constant change are:

- **Governance**. The framework must be robust and contained as a transferable skill.
- **Repeatable**. It needs to allow for constant change, which happens all the time.
- **Auditable**. It must be possible to measure real financial results.
- **Inclusive**. The change must involve all stakeholders.
- **Led strategy**. The change should be led by the organisation's leader and not operationally driven; companies that plan strategically will succeed over those that simply manage operationally.

An easy way to remember these is to use the acronym of **GRAIL** – this is the Holy GRAIL of leading constant change.

The system is also based on the philosophy of managing through employee participation in the company's decision making, using the four key performance concepts (outlined in Chapter 3), which in turn will result in an atmosphere of trust and fair play in the business:

- participative planning
- strategic appraisal
- financial understanding
- unbiased teams.

You are about to share a framework that has been used to create major international companies. Whether you are a business owner, a director or a senior manager, this framework can be used to develop your business, or indeed your department. Once installed, you own the process, and can repeat it periodically or whenever you are confronted by a change challenge.

When to use the framework

The decision to install a change management framework may be prompted by a number of different factors.

 Installing the framework

Do you need a change management framework?

Tick all that apply.

- Your business is facing pressures and you need to assess their impact and form a responsive plan. ☐
- You have become sceptical about the various change initiatives that have been running for a while, costing your business good money, promising much but delivering somewhat less. ☐
- You have become convinced that the answer to many issues lies within your workforce, but attempts to unlock this treasure chest have become thwarted for various reasons. ☐
- Your management team is busy driving the operational side of the business, but it seems to be always you who comes up with the new ideas. ☐
- You want to challenge your business to provide a catalyst for change, to re-energise the business and teams. ☐

- Shrinking margins or static revenue have given you an indication of external pressures, yet nothing seems to be addressing the problem. ☐
- Your strategy has or is about to change, but you need the company to get behind your plans – and quickly. ☐
- You feel disconnected from the front line and want to access this pool of talent, unfettered by management report lines and niceties. ☐
- You have become tired of change initiatives and need a robust and reliable framework that you can rely on. ☐
- Your management team needs to accept and take on greater responsibility for delivering results in a changing market. ☐
- You have taken over – or are about to take over – an operation, and need to hit the ground running. ☐
- You are about to merge or acquire another business and need to integrate it fast. ☐

If you do decide that you need to install a change framework, then first you need to consider various factors that will affect your success.

Above all, you need the authority to introduce the framework. This may sound obvious, but remember that this framework is holistic – it operates across a business in one operation. If you carry authority for only a part of the company, then you need to be aware that any cultural shift that you create (and you will create one) will have a knock-on effect in other parts of the business.

The grapevine in any company is an active (and potentially disruptive) mechanism for sharing things in an uncontrolled fashion. If you therefore create positive changes for just the one department that you control, then your colleagues will be knocking at your door very quickly asking why you have rocked the boat in their departments, and why you are improving things and creating an 'I want one too' response from their staff.

If you are responsible for a specific area, then your line manager or director will need to be briefed and accept the framework as the method for getting results. If possible, you should seek the agreement of the managing director, because they carry the authority needed across all business departments or subsidiaries.

Case study
Stakeholder consent

Recently I was working in a middle-sized council, which had ordered the framework for just one of their directorates. This area of the business needed prompt action to strengthen middle management, join up the workforce that appeared disenfranchised, optimise the budget for delivery of the front-line services and eliminate wasteful historic working practices that nobody wanted.

The work conducted was highly successful and the directorate was very satisfied. On this occasion the board had also given direct approval and so all was well – or so we thought. Upon review, the union representatives were unhappy that they had not been given the opportunity to approve this 'new management practice'. As a result, the board was asked to attend an elected members' meeting, where this framework was 'adopted' as an approved management tool in the future. By doing this, the unions were satisfied.

This case study illustrates the need to obtain consent with the key stakeholders before installing what may be considered to be a disruptive framework. Remember that the framework is all about change, and people often fear change.

You also need to be aware that, as the owner of this framework, your results may quickly outperform those previously obtained. If you have colleagues in other parts of the company, you may just inadvertently provoke a jealous reaction.

If you are the CEO, board director or owner of a company, then you have a slightly different problem. Introducing a change framework will invoke immediate suspicions, uncertainties and possible negative reactions in the immediate management team that reports to you. It is tempting to have a group discussion or presentation of this framework, in order to establish the 'buy in' from the team you will probably appoint as a change committee. But often the response to this from the management team is immediate resistance. This is because they are fearful of being in a situation where change possibly exposes them personally. So they come up with all kinds of excuses.

- Are we really ready for this?
- We haven't got the time to do this.
- We don't want to rock the boat when things are difficult as they are.
- Do we need this?
- Don't you trust us to manage as we are?

I've heard them all, and I have seen many directors give in to the protests and not proceed to install the framework. It is then a case of the tail wagging the dog.

 What excuses have you heard – or have you made yourself – against change?

Building the case for change

In order to install any framework for change, a case must therefore be made so that managers accept the way forwards. What you must do is prevent their becoming **change saboteurs**. You will need to spell out the situational need, gain acceptance of the need to change things, and outline just how difficult and unpredictable this is without a framework for change. In other words, you need to sell the decision that you have already made.

It may sound odd to have to sell the idea to a group of people you have employed to manage your business, but otherwise you will find that their hesitancy and negativity may derail your optimum result. I have watched aghast as senior directors of larger businesses have been told by their direct reports that they did not want to use a framework for change and that they were just 'too busy' for more change. Faced with a rebellious management team, the director retreated and accepted their word.

Consider what happens if you continue to operate your business as you are doing right now, and fail to gain acceptance for a change framework within the senior management teams.

- It will lead to **increased workload** in order to achieve employee engagement.
- It leaves the door open to **rejection** or behind-the-scenes sabotaging of any change plans that do not suit those impacted.
- It may expose a single manager to **increased work**, as opposed to a framework that regulates the fair and even allocation of work.
- It may lead to a **dilution of results** if the rules-based framework is not used to optimise the results.
- **Divide and conquer** tactics may be employed if there is no framework in place that protects the management team.
- Change results will almost certainly be achieved in a **slower timescale**, possibly jeopardising the organisation's financial results.
- The management team is seen as draconian **change imposers**, as opposed to change ambassadors using a framework.

Continued and future change programmes will be faster, simpler and require less work from a management team that uses a framework; the opposite is true if no framework exists.

🌐 *Framework presentation*

The results of any change programme will most certainly be greater with a framework for change, but deciding how and when to introduce it can be a fine balancing act. You need to build the case, build support from the trusted few, and then announce the collective idea to the wider team. But each company is different and the way in which you 'sell' the framework to your teams depends on your management style and the culture of your business.

In the next section of the book I will introduce the steps and rules that make up the framework for constant change. Remember, the steps are sequential, critical and not optional. They will lead you down the well-trodden path taken by many great business leaders, who have all used the framework very successfully over many years, with proven and published results.

Action points

- Print out the schematic of the framework for leading constant change and identify the steps and sequence.
- Use the schematic of the framework to share the outline with others.
- Print out the change audit document and complete the tick list.
- Decide that you will introduce this framework into your organisation.
- Work out the possible blockers to this within your own organisation.
- Devise a method and approach that will gain acceptance from within your organisation.

part two

The 15 steps to leading constant change

Step

Define your killer strategy for change

This step focuses on the need to think strategically. Surveys often find that about 80 per cent of organisations have defined their strategy, written down a vision statement for the company, and translated this into a mission statement or even a simple set of high-level objectives. Some have even published these on their website and framed them in their reception areas or board rooms.

But out of this 80 per cent who have done the headline work, only between 15 and 21 per cent actually use these strategy statements and objectives in the daily management of their businesses.

Yet companies that can demonstrably show this link and do manage in a strategic way are significantly higher performers than their counterparts – all those companies who say they are 'too busy with the daily problems' to worry about future strategy.

Thinking strategically

Strategic thinking is a critical aspect of driving a business and can mean the difference between excellence and mediocrity – or even failure. In a time of change, especially if you define change as constant, then this means all the time. Specifically, during the period where you are going to initiate a change planning session in your company, this strategic thinking becomes a vital component of your plan. Businesses start and stop with strategy.

So, a broad statement that 'We need to change' works just about as well as 'I want you to work harder'. Without specific data and references to *what* exactly you want to change, then the outcome could be just about anything.

As people in an organisation, you need to understand just what is being asked of you in order to change things. To do this, you need to know where you are headed. If you board an aeroplane with no idea of where it is going, you may feel a little uneasy, wondering if you'll like where you are going – and how you can get back again if you don't like it.

The same is true of change in companies. As a business leader, your role is to define and set the direction of the business, by:

- defining the business within its markets;
- ensuring you have sufficient means and resources to get where you want to go;
- plotting a course to arrive on time and within your resource limits.

If at this stage your defined strategy is not clear, or is in need of a refresh, then you need to examine and audit your strategy (see Chapter 1). Use the PEST analysis and the audit tools to take a new look at your markets, legislation affecting you, technology and competition. Don't forget the customer – since it is the customer, not the ego of the company, that will determine future success.

If you are intending to reassess, then don't lose the opportunity to gather intelligence and data from a diverse team within your company. By including them, you will raise awareness, create goodwill by inclusion, gather new data and expand your thinking outside your comfort zone (your usual team or teams).

If you are comfortable that your strategy is defined and good for purpose, then you are ready to initiate Step 1 of this change framework.

Creating a keynote speech

The purpose of Step 1 is to create a **keynote speech** of change. This is a one- or two-sided A4 document that will capture in words your vision and key objectives, and then translate that into a small number of defined measures that can be understood by everyone in your company.

Case study
Getting your message across

A few years ago I was working with the Derbyshire Fire and Rescue Service, which had an inspirational leader at the time. He constructed a keynote speech that said that 'We want an organisation of excellence', which for a CEO was a perfectly understandable statement. For his immediate senior leadership team, the equivalent to a board of directors, this was also an understandable statement. Move to the senior management team however, and they started to add statements such as 'and this must mean that ...'. They understood the statement, but wanted to contextualise it with quantifiable measures in their departments. By the time the message reached the fire stations, the word 'excellence' had little meaning, and to the fire fighters themselves it meant absolutely nothing. The fire was either blazing or it was out. There was no concept of an excellent fire or an excellent amount of water to put it out.

The CEO kept his headline statement. It was after all his signature and a mark of his good leadership, which few disputed. But he then set about adding context to the keynote speech, which is exactly what is needed.

The keynote speech should have no more than six key points to contextualise the vision – this is the maximum that can be understood at any one time. It is often useful to produce a bullet point list, for example:

- To seek out and reduce waste wherever we find it.
- To start to think about new ways of working to meet the needs of our customers.

- To increase our turnover by £1 million next year by winning new customers.
- To introduce a new range of products in xxx area.
- To reorganise the distribution area to allow faster turnaround of orders.
- To collaborate with a partner who specialises in IT, in order to be competitive in the next five years.

So should a keynote speech be just a motivational speech? My answer is no, but it does need to be an honest speech that gets positive attention. The key principle is to *be honest*. I have worked with many organisations who want to spell out the good things, and extol the benefits of the company or products. But your people know already if profits are down, budgets are halved, a key client has been lost, or the products are being out-boxed by your competitors. If you try to gloss over these subjects or pretend they are not happening, then you will fail to get the attention of the workforce. They will immediately label the speech as a sham, just another 'management thing'. You will not get their attention, and the exercise will become more difficult as a result.

Case study
Being honest

A local council was undergoing a complete staff restructure. Jobs were being lost to redundancy, budgets had been slashed by eye-watering amounts, and the whole world order was being changed, when the director ordered a staff engagement exercise.

It is always difficult to know when best to introduce engagement. Is it before a restructure, to give everyone the heads-up? Is it after a restructure, when colleagues have been lost and people's motivation is rock bottom? Or is it during the change process, when the director can take the opportunity to try to offer support, understanding that the pain isn't over yet?

The decision in this council was taken to engage with staff before completion of the restructure. A keynote speech was devised that began by acknowledging and offering empathy for the problems caused by restructure. These problems were not the personal fault of the directors, but the human touch – the apology they wove into the opening paragraph – was very well received. The wider workforce saw the directors as human beings, not just 'suits'. Perhaps the restructure was not a completely heartless process after all. The speech talked about the need to reshape the organisation, pick up the pieces and focus on just a few points, including protecting front-line services, fixing disjointed processes, consolidating workspace into smaller offices, and ensuring budgets were cut by wastage reduction before jobs were lost. This led to the strapline of 'Cut costs before jobs', which became a rallying call for the organisation and delivered many positive outcomes.

 What would you include in a keynote speech for change in your own organisation?

To create a convincing keynote speech, here are some tips.

- Make sure you 'speak' to the people – don't write a report.
- Start with an honest appraisal of the situation that you need to address.
- Own up to problems, issues and mistakes – the human touch is very powerful.
- Showcase successes, and thank staff for efforts so far.
- List five or six key bullet points of what you want to achieve.
- Make sure the language and words you choose are understandable by everyone in your business.
- If necessary, write two or more versions, changing the wording for specific areas of your business. A single speech may not be suitable for the boardroom as well as the manual workers.

- Try to end with a rallying message.
- Ask your teams for help – it's a very powerful motivator, and people like to help.

 Example keynote speech

The example of a keynote speech on the website provides more ideas or prompts for you. It also includes standard sentences to add on to the end of the keynote speech. (These refer to red boxes, which are dealt with in detail in Step 4, and the timescale for feedback, which could be between four and seven weeks from the start of the announcement of change in Step 3.)

Step 1 summary

By the end of this step you will have:

- drafted a keynote speech of strategic intent, which reaches out to all stakeholders and starts the process of engagement – a critical component of any change planning.

Step

2

Assemble your ninja change planning team

This step focuses on your appointed **change planning team**, and explains how your appointed team can very rapidly be developed to become your force for constant change management within the framework.

The change planning team consists of the people you have selected to drive this framework – the people who will take the leading role in managing the change. They need to be properly instructed and properly supported. If you fail to invest in this team at this time, then you risk the outcome of the planned or desired change.

Building a team

To prepare their teams, many organisations immediately think of an 'away day' – a chance to take their team off site, away from the business (usually somewhere nice), and to make them feel more appreciated. The idea is to have open discussions about the business, ask questions and formulate strategic plans. The idea is right, in so far as it creates a hiatus – a break from operations and an attempt to focus on the strategy. Properly planned, this can be an effective way of building a team, focusing on the strategic planning as opposed to operational needs.

However, since these days are usually reserved for the board of directors or senior management, they are often seen by others in the organisation as a 'management jolly'. And it is questionable just how much these events create a 'team'. Teams are built around many things, and an annual strategic planning session is only that: an annual event with only simple interaction that is quickly forgotten once back in the thick of things.

There is another way.

- Identify the team that you want to authorise to become the change planning team.
- Introduce them to the cause and requirements of change – this in itself creates a gelling effect, as people bond through adversarial conditions (such as the threat of change).
- Provide four team-training workshops. These are one-day, off-site events, which are run during the period when the keynote speech is announced and published and the red boxes (see Step 4) are collecting data.

When a team is created it usually goes through the classic team-building stages of **forming**, **storming**, **norming** and **performing**. The four workshops provide a platform for this to take place. Gradually the team bonds together because of a common responsibility to ensure the framework is enacted and a successful outcome is achieved.

Running workshops

The learning and delivery style of the workshops needs to be relaxed. They are usually facilitated by an external consultant, who is able to provide a non-invasive lead – there will be a very different result if the director or CEO leads these sessions. The subjects of the workshops are flexible, but the four cornerstones of managing and directing any organisation are:

- leading change
- finance
- planning
- organising.

Some clients like to insert technical content or sales content, to improve the team's understanding in these subjects. This may provide team-based learning, but it is important not to alienate individuals who have non-technical or non-sales roles and may feel disconnected from such subjects. Always include finance – even if this is the only workshop you ever run this year, for any reason! Finance is the keystone in the effectiveness of any manager, as Step 6 will demonstrate.

If the style of the workshops is right, then a highly interactive environment is established to provide the managers with the ability to discuss the business from every angle. These workshops are a chance to dig into the business – to take a fresh look at the mechanics, issues, strategies and operational pressures. It is also possible to discuss all areas of the business, not just each person's own department.

I have run many of these workshops and seen how a team comes together over the four sessions. Some teams may have been together for years, and yet when they are given this unique opportunity to attend a learning workshop, and encouraged to take part in open discussion, somehow the team is taken to a whole new level. Very often significant problems have been solved by discussions with the whole team in this kind of workshop.

Case study
Learning together

A great example of teamwork is shown by a manufacturer of an electric motor that is used inside mining equipment. The company had been hugely successful throughout a long recession, as it exported much of what it made to the still expanding economies of the East. Yet it had a problem; it could not make motors fast enough. Many of us would laugh and say what a great problem, but it threatened the survival of the business.

The orders were coming in thick and fast, but the issue was of course cash flow. Once an order was taken, the materials were ordered, payable on 45–60 days to the supplier. The customer paid FOB (freight on board) plus 30 days, which is a reasonable arrangement. The problem was that it was taking 14 weeks to

▶

make the product. The suppliers were paid on day 60, but the cash from the customers was not received for up to 115 days later. Every order taken was draining cash.

In a 'Finance for non-finance managers' workshop, this was a hot subject. For the first time, all the managers were asked to explain what was happening. The result was that the team talked about contracting, sales lead times, suppliers and stock holding. Of course the discussions focused on the factory build time. When challenged, it was admitted and agreed by the whole team that to make just one motor could take just 2 weeks not 14, but the factory bottlenecks were the entire issue. When asked to unpick this subject, several managers offered insights and explanations, and the focus settled on the electric oven as being the single largest bottleneck, as coils for the motors could only be cooked in the morning. It turned out that the electricity supply to the whole building was of inadequate capacity, so the ovens could only be used for half the time. The team tested various alternatives, such as upgrading the supply, alternating shifts, relocating the ovens to another building, and so on.

The entire supply chain was discussed, but to no avail. It was just one of those things that appeared insurmountable. Until one of the managers, nothing to do with the factory, asked the great question – could we use a gas oven as well, to improve workflow? For a very small investment, this bottleneck was relieved and resolved, immediately stripping weeks out of the production cycle and thereby accelerating cash flow.

It started as a finance discussion, and ended as a finance discussion, but the bit in the middle was pure magic!

To understand the importance of these workshops, and why teams need the common development platform that the workshops provide, we need to go back to the findings from the Stanford Research Institute that were so contentious they could not be published (see Chapter 2). This noted that with the inevitable demise of the centralised corporate planner, the activity of planning out the organisation and its resources has fallen to the senior functional executives. But this is full of problems, notably that managers are not trained for the task.

In many organisations, senior appointments are made from within, yet most of these appointments come with little or no training. Instead of a senior manager being able to invest 25–30 per cent of their time planning and thinking about the business, many will over-supervise daily operations. This makes them very busy doing the wrong things, and therefore unable to plan correctly.

Unable to plan the base business effectively and then separately plan the developing business, they prefer to leave planning to last, or upwards delegate it in some way to the finance director. With little formal support from the manager, then any plans lack the quality they need. The vicious circle goes around at dizzying speed, and businesses fail to plan or indeed operate strategically at the level at which there is maximum impact.

 Four workshops for learning

The website offers a series of PowerPoint presentations that provide you with some ideas for the content and scope of the learning workshops. The broad subject titles should provide some direction for your designated facilitator or trainer.

Creating a change planning team

The change planning team is that small group of selected people who will drive the change framework within your organisation and take responsibility for the process and the work that will result. I sometimes refer to them as the change committee, the change planning team, the tiger team – or even the ninja team!

I strongly suggest that, even if the people are simply the same as the senior management team, do not refer to them like that in this context of leading change – call them something different. A ninja team may be a cliché, but you can think of your own appropriate alternative.

It is important that the group of people are selected in the right way and for the right reasons.

- You should select them proactively, and not by default of their being a senior manager.
- Speak to them individually, one to one, explaining what is needed from them, and asking them for a personal affirmation – a commitment from them – to support the work and take on board the change authority.
- Make sure they agree that the change-related work will have total transparency within the company.
- Tell them that some additional effort may be needed above that of the 'day job'.
- Assure them that they will have your delegated authority and trust to drive this change framework.
- Make sure they have sufficient authority in the company to interface successfully across all departments.
- Let them know that you see their participation in this team as promotion in the business – something special in recognition of their skills and experience.

 Change planning team interview and acceptance contract

If you select your team randomly, or by default of position or situation, then you may dilute its possible outcomes. To understand why this is important, take another look at the distributive justice model, and the factors that provide positive feeds to the individual – such as recognition, opportunity for advancement, time with the boss, developmental work, appreciation of self (see Chapter 2). This is an opportunity for the individual, so make sure they understand this.

Unfortunately I have often witnessed a director or CEO who wants to strengthen the management team, and so simply nominates them for the task. While the intention may be good, any recruitment of team members must be done in a one-to-one interview, and not simply by automatic acceptance. Perhaps the worst situation I have experienced was the one where I was given assurance of the team selection, the keynote speech was written, and the team was assembled for the first piece of work. But when I opened the working meeting, I was told by the team that they had absolutely no idea why they were there, and that the CEO had used an Outlook invite to establish this meeting – with no clue or brief as to why!

There are also some individuals you would *not* invite to take part in the change planning team. These are people who:

- are about to retire or leave the business within three months of this programme being run;
- are too junior in the business, and therefore lack the daily authority to make things happen and initiate change projects;
- are part time, and therefore lack the time to drive the work afterwards;
- have asked specifically not to take part.

Here are some questions you might ask when setting up a team.

- **Can I, as a director or CEO, take an active part?** Yes, you can, although you will need to be sensitive to the fact that one of the framework rules is that nobody has any status or superior authority during the working sessions. You will also need to go the extra mile to show that this is true, or risk subduing your team.
- **Can I appoint non-managers or managers-in-training to the team?** Yes, you can. This can be an excellent forum to test out possible succession managers or trainee managers and watch them in action. But the final team must be made up of people who are sufficiently authorised to complete the planned work afterwards.

- **Should I have representation from all parts of the organisation?** It is an advantage to have a diverse representation, so this should be a selection criterion, but do not appoint a person just to fulfil this ideal.

- **The union representatives want to take part – should I let them?** I have always worked successfully with union representatives, and will often invite them to come to the working sessions, as observers only, to show them how the principle of fairness is at work. This framework sits well with their member representation, once they understand how it works. However, I would suggest that union representatives should not be default appointed, unless of course they meet the criteria.

- **A certain manager is always awkward and obstructive – shall I exclude that person?** Absolutely not! Examine the possible reasons why they are being obstructive. I have worked with teams where one or more members have been described in many negative ways at the start, yet once the framework is used, they will sometimes outperform the team 'stars'. The framework uses rule-based events, and so individuals are swept along by the process. With threats and fears removed, they often find the space to blossom.

- **I have a person who will be demotivated if I don't include them, but they are not my first choice – what now?** You have to balance your need to maintain support across the organisation and the need to appoint the very best team you can. This is a selection process, not just a generic management team exercise. There are certain stated requirements to join the team, and to gain understanding and agreement. Sometimes a way round is to soften rejection with phrases like 'I do think you have a lot on right now, and I'm worried I may overload you if you join this change planning team; could I perhaps count on your support once the outcomes are identified, and free your time at this stage?' The style and approach must be your own, but be clear – this framework requires your best team to get the best results.

- **What is the minimum and maximum number of people on this team?** In my experience I have worked with teams as small as 4, but this was in a very small business of only 30 people. Most of my assignments have worked with teams averaging 9, but I have also worked with a team of 14. There is no stock answer to this question, except to say that if your company is large then it may be an advantage to have a larger group of appointed change planning team members, but I would suggest that up to 15 is a maximum for effective working.
- **How much time will be required by each person appointed?** The core time needed is approximately 6–7 days of time, spread over 6–8 weeks. Thereafter, they have an ongoing responsibility to monitor and report on (but not necessarily do) the work and change projects identified by the framework outcomes.

Combining Steps 1 and 2

To bring these first two steps together, you need to brief the selected team in the workings of the change framework, and allow the team to appraise the suggested keynote speech, encouraging them to add, delete or amend any aspect (with your agreement).

By involving the team in this way, the team is able to:

- understand the reasons for the change framework;
- understand your thinking through the draft keynote speech;
- adopt the language and content of the keynote speech as its own.

Conclude this exercise by asking each team member to sign a separate copy of the final keynote speech, so giving their authority to issue it as a true representation of the team and their views. This cements their commitment to the change programme.

Step 2 summary

By the end of this step you will have:

- carefully selected and established your change planning team;
- defined the strategy;
- briefed the team in order to gain their buy-in and acceptance of the changes planned.

Step

3

Over-communicate the strategy

This step focuses on the need to 'unstick' the organisational meme, and provide the means for your valued people to move forwards with your business – though remember that people-based change will always lag process-based change.

Making people part of the plan

In earlier chapters I emphasised how important it is to make people part of the plan. As a member of the senior team, you could choose to calculate the changes and developments needed in your organisation and then simply impose them on the workforce. The acceptance factor may be a little low, but at least this method is quick and trouble free!

But of course the real trouble will start when you try to implement the changes without prior agreement. If you want sustainable and successful results, it is vital that you engage your staff and stakeholders.

> *"Habit is habit and not to be flung out of the window but coaxed downstairs a step at a time."*
>
> MARK TWAIN, *PUDD'NHEAD WILSON*, 1894

To create the rally call within your company, it is necessary to share the big picture. So first you should publish the keynote speech for change and encourage the whole organisation to start talking about it. Your task, and that of the selected change planning team appointed by you, is to expose every single person to the keynote speech of change.

Sharing the keynote speech offers everyone a heads-up that things are about to change – and that there is no option to do nothing. This is not as crude as showing people a burning bridge in order to move forwards, but rather it is an opportunity to share with them the aspiration to improve and make changes, and invite everyone to take part.

At this stage there will be the obvious dissenters, and those who do not want to change, but against that there will be a rising tide of those who accept that change is coming and want to be involved, as opposed to side-lined and excluded.

Repeating the message

It has been suggested that in order for a message or piece of instruction to be completely and fully understood, it is necessary to present it in seven ways, at seven different times: the **7 × 7 matrix** of communication. By repeating the message in various ways you can:

- overcome the mental filters that people apply;
- overcome selective memories;
- appeal to people in different ways;
- reinforce the message by repetition;
- allow unspoken rejection to become acceptance.

Remember, it is not enough to tell it once or twice and think people will accept, believe or understand what it is you are telling them.

How you could communicate the keynote speech to all staff:

- Written form:
  - emails
  - memos
  - organisational intranet
  - personal letters in payslips
  - internal newsletter.
- Face to face or verbally:
  - team meetings
  - informal meetings
  - one-to-one meetings
  - general discussions.

The seven different times will be possible because the communication process I am recommending will continue for between four and seven weeks (as described in Step 4).

 How many different ways do you commonly use to communicate to your team?

Using the right language

In Step 1 I referred to the different levels of understanding within departments or layers of your business. You may need to adjust your language to suit the recipient, without losing the message.

So, in the case of the fire fighters (in Step 1), the word 'excellence' was translated into 'getting it right first time', 'being efficient and highly trained' or 'being the best that we can'. The message still contained the word 'excellence', but the change planning team added 'which means that …' lines, to allow better understanding in the context of the job role.

Communication is critical when leading change. If insufficient effort goes in, then the outcomes will be more difficult to deliver. For a little bit of effort, this will have an exponentially positive effect on delivering changes later.

Step 3 summary

By the end of this step you will have:

- established your communications strategy, which is probably the most important aspect of any engagement exercise.

Step

4

Really engage your staff

This step focuses on communication, and how it is never a one-way discussion. Unfortunately, engagement can be difficult and is often fraught with interpersonal issues of control and response.

Earlier I emphasised the importance of participative planning (see Chapter 3), which is what Step 4 is all about. The participative planning approach does away with unpopular focus groups, ineffective or divisive surveys, and various other techniques that only partially work. Instead, everyone in the company is given a copy of the change vision: the keynote speech of change.

Now you are about to ask the single most powerful question of all. It is a question that has no limits, no boundaries and no requirement to use fancy language – or even to have a correct answer.

Yet the question will engage your staff like no other, and provide you with information that is honest, direct, powerful and far-reaching. It can provide ideas that lead to new products, new customers, reduction of your cost base and the willing sacrifice of wasteful activity and time.

The question you are now going ask your staff and stakeholders is simply this: 'What do you think?'

Engaging everyone

The answers to the question are given back to you by your employees and stakeholders using the **planning issue** form (Form1), either by online submission or in paper form posted in red metal post boxes placed all round your organisation (see Figure S4.1). Most importantly, the forms and the information on them are all anonymous.

 *'Have your say' template*

Figure S4.1 The completed Form1s are posted in a bright post box

The anonymity is extremely powerful. It allows truthful feedback to be provided by every individual, regardless of their confidence, vocabulary skills, knowledge or expertise. It allows people to ask questions and comment across the whole business – not just in their own areas. It provides a means to tell it how it is, without the information being discarded, rejected, changed or sanitised for line management consumption.

Above all, it makes the process fair – remember that word, that powerful driver? It is fair that everyone has an equal voice, untainted by others, and is given equal weighting and credibility. If you look at a Form1 submission, you will have no clue as to its origin – it could be from the CEO, a factory worker, a manager, an expert, an administrator, a delivery person, a designer …

Importantly, you cannot discriminate against an anonymous submission. Its origins are unknown: the person who has filled it in might be from any ethnic origin, able-bodied or less abled, male or female, a new recruit or an experienced employee, young or old – all unknown.

It is the most inclusive method of engagement that I have ever come across. It remains completely non-threatening, is completely fair and provides the most exciting opportunity to 'tell it how it really is' that people may ever be offered.

How Form1 works

This is no ordinary form. It has been designed with people psychology in mind, so people are comfortable with filling it in.

Team Action Management

TAM
Team Action Management

Delivers Successful Change And Increased Performance
To All People Based Organisations

Form 1: Your views/opinions

Please give a short title

Decide which box your title refers to and tick only 1

PRESENT	OR	FUTURE	
Strength	☐	Opportunity	☐
Fault	☐	Threat	☐

· Statement of your view or opinion – 1 per form please

_____
_____
_____
_____
_____

· Do you want to give an example?

_____
_____
_____
_____
_____

· What could be done

_____
_____
_____
_____
_____

Unleashing the power

TAM Uk Plc © 2008 Team Action Management ™

Figure S4.2 Form1: Planning issue

Form1: Planning issue

Filling in Form1

- Give the issue a short title – just a broad title to identify the issue.

- Tick one box to show whether the issue is a strength, a fault, an opportunity or a threat.

- Write a short description of the problem or potential improvement. This can be as informal as you like – people have even drawn pictures here!

- Provide an example on which this is based. This is optional, but will provide more information about the issue.

- Add any suggestions for improvements. Again, this is optional, but can be helpful.

- Remember, only one issue per form, but you can fill in as many forms as you want.

- Then post the form in the boxes provided.

Note that there is no identity to the writer, but if there are concerns about handwriting recognition, then refer to the example online Form1 on the **www.managingconstantchange.co.uk** website.

Respecting the information

The information that people provide on the planning issue form is personal to them. It is not the summary page from a team meeting, or something that a small committee may want to write up. It is a comment from an individual, a real person, who is using anonymity to give the organisation a gift. The gift is simple: it is a part of that person and their feelings and thinking. It has emotion attached to it – while writing it, and especially when posting it irretrievably into the red collection boxes.

In fact it may take a couple of weeks for people to summon the courage to fill in a form in the first place, which is precisely why I advocate four to seven weeks of data collection.

Case study
Using the boxes correctly

In one manufacturing environment I personally went in after a couple of weeks to see how the boxes were filling up. The answer was – they weren't. I walked around and encouraged every operator to get involved: 'What you don't tell us, we can do nothing about', I told them. And with this genuine encouragement, they started completing Form1s across a wide range of subjects. The box filled up quickly and the departmental manager called me to tell me. I said to him that if he wanted to swap the box for an empty one, he should call the union representative, and one or two randomly selected engineers, and have them witness the removal of the (locked) box from the shop floor to a place of safe keeping, then tape up the postal slot with duct tape. Then he should place an empty box in its place. This may sound rather theatrical, but it is a necessary demonstration of consideration and confidentiality.

The manager must have thought about this for a while, decided it was silly and simply swapped the box for an empty one during a coffee break. It took about half an hour for an engineer to notice the box was empty. Within 20 minutes the shop floor had called a stop to production and tools were downed. The staff believed their confidential comments had been removed by 'management' and would be read selectively (with unwanted comments discarded). The contract of confidentiality and anonymity had been breached. It was a full shift before normal working was resumed – and only after a visit from me and the MD to the shop floor with the full (locked and untampered) box produced as evidence.

Another client had a large team of over 100 onsite operators over eight locations, working in landscape and litter control within a council. The rollout of the keynote speech and the red boxes was an entertaining exercise, since it took place in Portakabins with teams of high-viz-clad operators with fairly direct language and a heightened excitement at the prospect of 'telling them how it is.'

The anonymity and box security were described, and the boxes were placed in canteen and clocking on/off areas for ease of access.

It was only a week into the six-week data collection exercise that I received the early morning phone call. 'I am from the council', he said. 'We have loads of Form1s here, but we don't trust the red boxes.' I asked him why. 'Because we think management can get their fingers in the postal slot and pick out the forms to read when we aren't there,' came the reply. 'In fact, we've tested it, so we know it can be done if you have skinny fingers.' And so we arranged to meet, behind the big tree a street away from the town hall, whereupon a shifty looking guy in a high-viz vest produced around 140 completed Form1s and told me to keep them safe. This was repeated throughout the six weeks that followed.

I used to think this type of behaviour was something left behind in the playground, until I realised that the workspace is in fact a playground. In many organisations this can be the first time anyone has ever asked the staff to give anonymous information, and I thought that it would be easy for them. Not so. The anonymity places emotional pressure on the individual and a higher level of responsibility to convey the right information.

You may be forgiven for thinking that with anonymity would come a barrage of bad language, accusations, cheap shots at managers and unreasonable demands for pay and conditions. In reality I have not come across this with my clients. Yes, I've seen a lot of working condition issues, many health and safety breaches and concerns, a few counts of bullying or inappropriate behaviour, but the cheap shots and disparaging comments can be counted on one hand.

Case study
Positive feedback

While working with a heavy engineering company a few years ago, the machine operators literally would not speak to me. They just nodded, or made a guttural noise in response to my asking them to complete Form1s or explaining the keynote speech of change (which they had placed carefully on the wall next to the page-three pin-up calendar). I was a little concerned that one of the change planning team attended the working sessions with his bandana still around his head, and I did wonder just what if anything I would get from the red boxes. But when they were opened, imagine my surprise to find gems of information – suggestions to improve process, materials handling, and a major health and safety issue. One team even volunteered to come in at the weekend (for no overtime or pay) to re-organise the machinery to create a better workflow.

From the feedback you get, and the more the merrier, you will have information, perspectives, issues, opportunities and simply gems of ideas that you will never obtain by any other engagement means.

Putting the process into action

Clients often have a number of questions about this engagement step of the change framework.

 *Form1 checklist*

- **When do I put the red boxes and Form1s into the working environment?** The red boxes, dressed with the 'Have your say' livery, are placed in the organisation at the same time that you announce, publish and communicate the keynote speech of change. Make sure you deploy enough boxes and place them where people want them – not where you think they should go. Your staff and stakeholders need to feel they own the red-box process.

- **Why do they stay out for four to seven weeks?** This allows people to get used to the boxes, discuss them, think of things to say, and then be courageous enough to fill in some forms. There is always a crowding effect: when one person admits to filling in a few Form1s then the rest will follow.

- **Can this time be shorter, like two weeks for example?** It can be shorter. In emergency turnaround conditions I have been known to give people 24 hours to respond, but then the 'burning bridge' concept exists, and emotions run high. To lead constant change, then, a slower, more considerate pace is needed – people need to feel they have a dignified time to respond.

- **Do the boxes need to be red?** The boxes represent something new and different in the workplace, and simply need to stand out. One of my clients sprayed them all bright yellow to make them stand out – the choice is yours.

- **What are the characteristics of the collection box?** Only that they are securely locked and cannot be accessed easily by anyone. One client did ask that they be bolted to a frame within the factory to avoid the 'workers putting them in the crusher' – a great example of management overreaction to red boxes and Form1s!

- **Can we just leave the boxes out all the time?** No. The boxes and the psychology of engagement are set around a defined timescale, which is followed up by specific action as described in the steps that follow. If you leave them out all the time, you will lose the engagement and significantly compromise any future attempts to repeat this framework.

- **So how often do we repeat this programme?** Just like a football that stops rolling after being kicked, the programme will come to a halt unless it is repeated. Most of my clients choose to do this annually; some also have an interim six-month programme when substantial changes are required or are forced upon them.

- **What happens at the end of the collection period?** I will outline the procedures in later steps, but basically the boxes are removed in full sight of staff, then locked away for 12–24 hours, or until the contents are taken under lock and key into the main change planning session.

- **How many blank forms do we need per box?** Placing a small pile of Form1s next to the box is a good way of making it easy for everyone to complete. One client additionally sent out five forms in wage slips to every employee as a prompt. The number of Form1s returned in any situation varies hugely, from 0.6 to 5 times the number of staff. As you will see in later steps, the more forms that are returned, the greater the level of engagement. It doesn't matter what they say at this stage – just encourage multiple forms per person, and keep the piles of blanks topped up in each area.

- **We operate in a unionised environment – do you have any tips?** Involve the unions from the start. Unions should always be invited to observe this framework in action, as it allays any fears of 'management manipulation' or underhand practices. This framework is totally transparent, and often the only way to allow people to engage and use the Form1 process is to gain the consent of the unions. Once they understand the entire process, they are usually one of your best assets, as they encourage staff to participate.

- **Is this really a suggestion scheme?** No, absolutely not. This is a data entry point to a change framework. It stays available for a short space of time and is totally anonymous. It collects data around a rallying cry for change. Do not confuse this with a passive, usually unmanaged means of collecting ideas and suggestions (often of an operational nature).

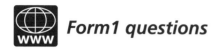 *Form1 questions*

The staff may also have some questions about the Form1 process.

- **Do you fix every issue?** No, we never promise to fix any issue. The opportunity to 'have your say' is just that. We cannot promise to fix an issue, as one form may say one thing and the next contradict it.

- **Who reads the forms?** The change planning team will all read every form.

- **So, if you don't like what's written, you just throw it away?** The rules of this change framework mean that forms cannot be thrown away. Every form submitted will be used and accepted, and will be part of the final plan in some way.

- **So can I track where my form has gone to and which plan it ended up in?** No, we don't track each form to the outcome – this would take far too much time and would add no value to the plan.

- **Will anything actually happen, or will it go quiet, just like before?** This framework is a programme of action, and intended actions will be announced to everyone after the change planning session.

- **So, if my issue isn't definitely going to get fixed, why bother?** You can choose to share your views, and maybe, with the collective returns from your colleagues, action will result. As you appreciate, not everything can happen perfectly for everybody – this is a business – but the fairest thing we can do is offer you an anonymous voice in the change planning session room. Remember, what you don't tell us, we can do nothing about.

Step 4 summary

By the end of this step you will have:

- asked people to engage, so now you must deliver an outcome – or suffer instant disengagement; your journey has now started and there is no turning back!

Step

5

Understand your change plan

The next four steps of the change framework focus on the change planning team itself and how they will deal with the entire change programme in the space of just two days (or three days, if the organisation has over 1,000 staff). They will build you a plan that is robust, supported, acceptable at the point of impact and highly efficient – and all linked to your strategy.

The change planning team must, above all, **understand the change plan**. So this is the subject of the first learning workshop.

The facilitator of the workshop needs to work through a number of stages.

- Invite the CEO or senior business sponsor of the change programme to attend – even if it is only for 10 minutes at the very start. This figure needs to confirm to the team that:
  - they have been purposefully selected for this important role;
  - they have delegated authority to drive this framework;
  - they have the confidence of the board;
  - their work and reports will become part of the board review each month;
  - they need to be bold, and not held back by the past;
  - each team member has one voice and there is no authority in the room;
  - the future culture of the business is in their hands – one of fairness, trust, performance and results.
- Explain that the team is here to chalk and talk: this will be a highly interactive discussion workshop, interspersed with modules of learning.
- Describe the framework in sufficient detail for each attendee to be clear about what is going to happen and when (using a PowerPoint presentation).

- Ensure that the keynote speech is available and then open it up to discussion (the team will already have seen an earlier draft in Step 1). Allow interpretation and encourage examples of context.

- Ask the team to recount their experiences of the workforce reaction to the keynote speech.

- Ask them about the red box collection process – how this has been received in the company.

- Encourage the team to add their own ideas, using Form1s – tell the team that you will expect at least a dozen Form1s from each of them during the workshops. The use of the Form1 is critical here: unless the directors and change planning team input to this process, then there is a danger that the feedback will be treated as workforce-only originated, and be perceived in some way as naïve or unimportant.

- Once the process of explaining the framework is complete, open up the session to questions. Encourage discussion of any areas of the business that are of interest, or may be the focus of or a challenge to the change programme.

At the end of this workshop, you need to give a rallying call to the team to continue to promote the Form1 – they need to encourage the entire workforce to complete and submit the forms. If a problem is encountered, or a situation discussed, then they should try using the little catchphrase 'Stick it on a Form1'.

By maximising feedback, the job of forming the output actions is made so much easier, because it demonstrates full engagement with all stakeholders. The worst scenario is if the red boxes/online portal are empty or very poorly fed, because this means the team has failed to engage at all.

Step 5 summary

By the end of this step you will have:

- concluded the briefing of your change planning team, which is now fully focused on the job in hand.

Step

6

Know where your profits come from

This step focuses on the need of the change planning team to **understand the finances**. During my 25-year career as director of many businesses, understanding finance and accounting has been absolutely critical. I am constantly amazed how many individuals occupy very senior positions in some major companies and yet have failed to invest in business finance training either for themselves or their senior teams.

To comply with the Companies Act in the UK, and its equivalent elsewhere in other countries, you have to understand money, so that you can spot fraud and misappropriation. In addition, in the day-to-day operations of the business, ignorance of finance will cost the business dearly, leading to operational problems, loss of performance, and poor profit and cash flow.

In any senior management role a strategic finance course is vital – and a route to furthering your career. The finance workshop is not the place to look at issues of robust board reporting and governance. Instead, I will focus on those areas of finance that you and the team need to know – either as a manager or a director.

The manager and finance

The manager's role is to manage operations and the associated risk for the business. It is also their role to plan out future developments, and so a reasonable understanding of Excel as a simple analytical tool is desirable, otherwise too much reliance is placed on the finance department.

Financial questions for a manager

- In your profit and loss report, look at the revenue or income line. What are the fluctuations against previous months?

- Examine the materials and direct costs lines. As a percentage of sales, is there an upwards or downwards movement from previous months? If so, why? A small fluctuation may have little effect, but any trend can be significant, especially if it is downwards.

- Review the individual cost lines. Are there budget variations? What are the reasons for this? Are they simply due to errors, unexpected circumstances, or a failure in the budget planning process?

- In your area of responsibility, who has authority to purchase and issue instructions to purchase? Does this link in with your budget control, or is someone else able to spend your budget without asking?

- How do you know what budget is free, allocated or spent? How do you control this?

- Do you take part in the budget-setting process, or are the budgets simply imposed on you?

- How do you replan your budgets if something changes fundamentally?

- Do you understand the difference between an invoice with payment terms of 30 days and one with payment terms of 30 days net?

- Do you assess your customers and suppliers for financial stability on a regular basis?

- What is your plan in future to obtain the above information?

The director and finance

If you are an organisational director or equivalent, I'm going to assume that you have the skills to answer the questions above. So now I will include some questions about the basic measurements and reports that you should understand as a director, to comply with Companies Act, and to protect your business.

The amount of knowledge may appear onerous, but in a period of growth, consolidation or change it is this information and these skills that may mean the difference between success and failure.

Financial questions for a director

- Do you receive a regular profit and loss statement, balance sheet and a forward-looking cash flow forecast (based on qualified sales assumptions)? Even if you do receive such information, do you understand it, or do you delegate the whole finance matter to the finance director or controller?

- Do you have a graphical presentation of the gross margin fluctuations? This is vital, because just a few percentage shifts in gross margin can mean the difference between a profit and a loss, so any movement needs attention.

- Do you have sufficient cash in the forecast to meet the business needs?

- What are your stock days (the time it takes for stock to become a sale)? Too much stock tied up cash costs real money in warehousing and storage, insurance, handling, recording overheads, etc.

- What are your debtor days (the time it takes for your customers to pay you)? Many people think this is a 'best effort' exercise – a hit-and-miss thing – but this is the measure by which you control cash. It may not sound serious if you have a customer who spends £100,000 per month with you, but pays you 5 days late per month. But 5 × 12 months is 60 days per year where your business is effectively lending the customer £100,000 for nothing. Add a zero on the end and see what the effect is. Cash collection is a serious matter, and as a director you should ensure that cash collection and payment terms start with the sale quotation: make sure that the price offered to the customer and the payment terms are inextricably linked. This makes your job so much easier when you come to collect.

- Do you understand what your breakeven position is? You need to determine this as a hard sales number, or the number of widgets sold or made, and also know the time in the month when breakeven should take place.

- Can you read the balance sheet to indicate liquidity ratios?

- Do you know the difference between a balance sheet movement and a profit and loss item?

- Can you compare your balance sheet with that of a competitor and make comments?

- Do you understand what your return on capital employed (ROCE) percentage is?

I cannot stress enough the importance of this knowledge and understanding – for both managers and directors. It could be that an external course is beneficial, or perhaps a finance controller might train the whole management team.

Step 6 summary

By the end of this step you will have:

- ensured that your change planning team is conversant in finance and financial efficiency – which will have an instant and positive effect on your business.

Step

7

Plan by project

This step focuses on **project planning** and why this approach is vital to managing constant change.

Project management is like the single cell structure that builds into any kind of forward-looking management system. This step is not the place for a run-down of project management techniques, since there are many other books, publications and systems that can show you how project management works. However, they probably won't share why a specific approach to managing projects is necessary to create a GRAIL-compliant framework (as outlined in Chapter 3).

Looking after the base business and the development business

In any business, there are two parts:

- **Base business** is the business or activity that your business will perform if you just respond to existing customers, don't create new products or services, let the customer phones ring inbound only, and just sit tight.
- **Development business** is about creating new products or services, training your people, focusing on marketing, or trying to develop anything new.

Development business is needed to stay in business. This is because base business will always decline – the rate of this decline is specific to your business and your sector.

But even if you know this, and then say to your sales teams or customer-facing teams, 'I want more' or 'We must do better', they may be forgiven for looking confused. How much more of what, and better in what way?

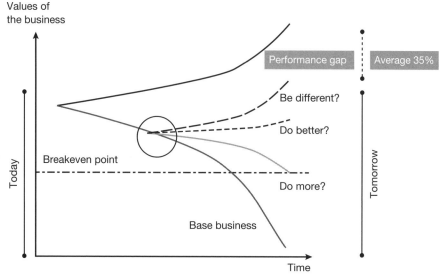

Figure S7.1 Measuring the base and development business

To be able to measure any kind of result, you need first to measure the base case, and then you need to measure the development case, to see if it works. Otherwise, your numbers may increase or decrease, but you will never fully understand why.

Figure S7.1 shows how a developing business is made up of the more bit, the better bit and the different bit. There is not a single event, but a series of projects and events that cumulatively make up the developing business.

So it is with managing constant change. The activity is focused into projects for development and change, and managed as a standard project would be, but with the change framework to push it along and to make it happen.

Step 7 summary

By the end of this step you will have:

- shown your change planning team how to differentiate between the today business and the business of tomorrow;
- made sure that the change planning team – and not just the board – is fully involved in proper strategic planning.

Step

Uncover how your business actually works

This step focuses on **organisational structure** and some of the fundamental weaknesses in the way that organisations are structured.

Organisational structures are usually the result of unhappy accidents, which simple evolve over time. How much of the following do you recognise in your own organisation?

- In the beginning, there is the **business leader**, owner or appointed person to build the business.
- They build the business by recognising the skills, abilities and interests of the first people appointed to the organisation. So a person who is interested in sales, or who are sales people, focuses on sales and then later becomes the manager or director of sales. But someone who is a great salesperson is not always the best person a business will ever have, and certainly may not be any good at managing people.
- The person in charge draws on their experiences from previous businesses, or otherwise asks someone else (usually their accountant, or a friend in another business), or reads a book on management.

This classic organisational model, or **theory of management**, was developed by the French mining engineer Henri Fayol in the 1870s. He believed work should be divided up between people with different specialisations, so he outlined a structure that had a chief director, to whom departments such as sales, operations and finance reported. Other theorists then added advice on the hierarchy between different areas, and added extra areas of responsibility like business development, human resources and technical departments.

- In this embryonic company the skills and limitations of the individuals employed have a large impact. For example, if the sales director has great technical skills, then the technical department might report through them – although this goes back to one of those unpublishable findings from the Stanford Research Institute about over-supervision (see Chapter 2).

- Once the company reaches a certain size, the structure of many people reporting to the MD has to give way to **departmental planning,** and lower management or supervisors are created.

- Little regard at this stage may be given to the customer or the end user of the product or service.

- Managers and directors see the opportunity to have more people report to them as a great way to build more importance, credibility and salary into their personal roles. This is how little empires spring up within businesses and knowledge sharing is reduced. After all, knowledge is power.

- 'My department' and 'my teams' become bargaining chips for privilege and power, to the point where you may find yourself negotiating internally for resources.

- Reporting becomes the currency of the departments, as they seek to justify their position, people and responsibilities through graphical reports and budgets.

- Apportioning new work, new projects and people becomes a jostling act between department managers, as each seeks to own or disown the optional work.

- If the company tries to downsize, each department immediately throws up barriers to protect their resources.

So over time the organisational structure changes. In addition, people may be asked to take on more work per person than ever before. Even if you are at a senior level, you may now be responsible for previously task-orientated matters, such as:

- typing your own work, using word processing and emails;
- scheduling your own meetings;
- juggling with enormous amounts of data and information.

It is also likely that you will take responsibility for a much more highly educated workforce. The nine-to-five, do-as-you-are-told approach is long gone.

Unfortunately, this often means that directors have become task-orientated 'do-ers' as opposed to strategists. They have little time for planning, and spend too much time managing the daily operations. In theory, senior management should spend 15–20 per cent of their time on planning and thinking, while directors should be able to set aside 30–35 per cent of their time for planning and strategy. In practice, this rarely ever happens.

 How much time can you set aside for planning and strategy?

Improving your organisational structure

Here are some tips on how to design an organisational structure that actually works.

ALWAYS

- **Group like work with one boss.** This makes the operations more efficient. However, if localisation of the work is the result of customer demands, then centralisation may not be desirable: make sure the customer needs are placed first.

- **Separate development from operational activities.** It is essential to separate the base business from the new development business in reporting terms. If reporting is mixed up then it is not possible to appreciate the difference and the effectiveness of developmental actions.

- **Keep within the maximum spans of control.** Spans of control are the number of direct reports that one person is reasonably expected to manage. In a factory or call centre (with many people doing the same work) it is possible for a span of 5–35 (optimal 15–35) subordinates per manager. At a more common level, with a manager of workers who perform different functions within a department or geography, this span of control should not exceed 7 (optimal 3–7).

- **Move activities higher in the company that are cash-flow sensitive**. This is critical to work allocation. To work out which of your activities are cash-flow sensitive, follow the instructions below. You will find that this is one of the most simple, yet most effective tools for an organisational structure audit, review and reform. Try it for yourself, than cascade it down to your teams.

 *Organisational audit*

Which tasks are cash-flow sensitive?

- Take a piece of paper and draw a table, as below – or use the template from the website.
- Now write down everything you do in a week. That's right – everything! Don't worry if the list goes over several pages, or is repeated.
- Against each and every task description, place an X in just one of the columns by answering the question: 'How close to cash flow is this action?' (Or, if you are in a not-for-profit environment: 'How close to customer service is this action?')
- Score each task as follows: 1 = high, 2 = medium (not directly related) and 3 = low (not connected).

TASK	3	2	1
Deal with emails		X	
Set up meeting	X		
Speak to IT about a problem	X		
Meet with prospective customer			X

TASK	3	2	1
Set up exhibition stand	X		
Attend seminar	X		
Write to building landlord		X	
Train a team member	X		
Order stationery	X		
Call prospects			X
Meet with supplier		X	
Arrange Christmas party	X		

- Now turn the paper 90 degrees to the left. This is what the scores mean:
  - Tasks that appear at the top row (the number 1s) are yours to have and own.
  - Tasks that appear in row 2 are yours to manage but not necessarily do.
  - Tasks in row 3 can all be delegated to others.

TASK	DEAL WITH EMAILS	SET UP MEETING	SPEAK TO IT ABOUT A PROBLEM	MEET WITH PROSPECTIVE CUSTOMER	SET UP EXHIBITION STAND	ATTEND SEMINAR	WRITE TO BUILDING LANDLORD	TRAIN A TEAM MEMBER	ORDER STATIONERY	CALL PROSPECTS	MEET WITH SUPPLIER	ARRANGE CHRISTMAS PARTY
1				X						X		
2	X						X				X	
3		X	X		X	X		X	X			X

- **Delegate items that are not cash-flow sensitive**. Delegating row 3 items will do two things:
  - It will free your time to concentrate on what is important – what is aligned to cash flow or customer service.
  - It will provide an easy list of developmental work for your reporting team. Don't forget, opportunities to do different or project-based work can be seen as a chance for positive engagement.

AVOID

- **One-over-one management relationships**. This may sound obvious, but I often see this in organisations that have simply evolved. It leads to wasted time in the management process, isolation for the employee, and should be avoided wherever possible.

- **Matrix management organisation**. Matrix management is popular in many businesses. For example, in retail brand selling a brand manager champions a certain brand and then uses the organisational resources to deliver. It is also evident in special project delivery for the same reasons. Here, the rules are defined and each person knows where they stand. But in a matrix organisation people have a 'dotted line' report to another function, parent company, subsidiary or management team. Where this occurs there is often confusion, split loyalties, wasted resources and an ineffective management style. Where matrix management is absolutely needed, then ensure the rules are very clear. Perhaps place an agreed stop date, to allow people to reassess any difficulties within a time frame. Make sure that managers know who is the line manager and who is the operations 'dotted line' – this is vital for performance reviews and resource allocations.

- **Centralising any functions that require people skills**. When some organisations reappraise their delivery channels they think that a good way to deliver the service to the customer for less money is to centralise or even automate the functions of interface. But don't ever forget that people buy from people, so the closer your service or products are to people, then the greater the need to maintain your people as an effective interface to your customers. Think about the rush to place banking call centres outside the UK, and the problems sometimes associated with this shift. So much so, that some organisations are now actually making a selling point of confirming a UK-based support function. You need real customer service managers to support you – and real people available who understand your local needs.

NEVER

- **Subcontract the 'heart' of the company**. As soon as you subcontract the heart of the operation, you lose the reason for being in business. It is the single factor that makes your business 'you', and the reason why your customers will identify with you and use your products and services.

- **Separate the MD from the responsibility of sales and cash flow**. I am often asked by MDs and directors (usually in a quiet place): 'How do we know what we are supposed to be doing'? It's actually a serious question. As the organisation grows and people and processes take over those things that the directors did when they started, or when a significant shift occurs in the operation or the markets, who tells the MD what to do with their time? Aspects of the role that should never be relinquished are the responsibility for sales (or customer service in the public sector) and cash flow. Even if others are responsible for the departments associated with both selling (or customer service) and cash, it is the MD who is ultimately responsible, and therefore who must maintain a keen watching brief over both these areas.

A different way of working

Finally, you need to consider the recent trend towards **agile working**. This is not simply working from home, although this is one facet of agile working. It is the recognition that:

- work is no longer a place – it is an activity;
- flexible working is a requested right for many employees;
- businesses can no longer afford to invest their capital in underutilised workspace;
- technology (mobile telephones, laptops, cloud computing, Voice Over Internet Protocol, etc.) increasingly allows people to work from other locations, be that a local work centre, supplier or customer premises, work hubs, home and so on.

Agile working is more than making your staff flexible in their work location, although estate costs are often a primary driver for such moves. However, remember that when a team member works away from the usual physical location you lose the daily contact with them. The relationship between the worker, the manager and the work is changed.

So If you aspire to agile working, then you must also embrace a new way of managing. This includes:

- focusing on output results, rather than simply being at a desk between 9.00 and 5.00;
- looking at how the work can be packaged (into projects for example) to provide assurance to both worker and manager of progress and achievement;
- examining the personal needs of both parties as to level and frequency of communication, and watching out for isolationism, which can hugely affect performance in a negative way.

If you are to gain the true benefits of agile working, then the rules of work need to be changed and agreed – otherwise you will find that a desk-shuffling exercise will cost you and your business dearly.

- Would agile working be appropriate for your own company?
- How would you ensure that managers could manage their remote teams?
- How could the remote teams do the work expected while still remaining connected to their work colleagues?

Skills workshops

These last four steps (Steps 5, 6, 7 and 8) have outlined the four key areas of change management development that are essential to a successful and proactive performing team:

- understanding the change plan;
- knowing where the profits come from;
- planning by project;
- uncovering how the business actually works.

 Four workshops for learning

The website provides PowerPoint materials to help formulate the skills workshops and take your change planning team on their learning journey. These workshops are not a precise event, in that the exact subjects discussed or taught are not critical to the success of the framework. The subjects I would personally consider essential are the leading change and the finance workshops, while the planning and organisational workshops are optional, but highly desirable.

If you are using an external training company, then they need to be fully versed in the framework. In this way you will be able to encourage the skills in your team that will make a positive difference to the business, as they move on to the next stage. It can also be useful to place a red collection box and a bunch of blank Form1s in the middle of the table before the workshops start, and then during discussions invite the team to record their comments and ideas in the box.

Step 8 summary

By the end of this step you will have:

- used the organisational audit to encourage your managers to question report-line efficiency;
- encouraged your managers to be more open to different styles of control;
- used the audit to analyse workloads so that managers can free up the time needed to drive the business instead of the detail;
- highlighted how improved delegation and shifting responsibility can allow greater staff engagement.

Step

9

Create a theatre for change

This step focuses on creating the best environment for the **change planning session** itself.

Remember, whenever you have promoted a team of people to be your change planning team, there will be a certain amount of fear and trepidation. They might be asking themselves:

- What happens if the team suggests something unpalatable?
- How will we overcome problems?
- Will we be exposed personally in any way?
- What happens next?

I always recommend that this change planning session is taken off site. This not only removes the usual distractions, but it also spells out that this is a serious business. It shows that the company is committed at the highest level, and that the team are the people the organisation has invested in, in order to make this change happen.

Over the years I have worked with some businesses that have gone the extra mile. Why rent a normal boring hotel conference room when for a small amount more you could have a showcase such as a historic castle or a remote location with fantastic views? After all, when making changes, changing the environment can be inspirational.

Recently I ran a change planning session for a relatively small business, which chose to hold the event in a hotel conference room. Afterwards, a director said to me, 'I really wish I'd invested in somewhere a bit different for this session. I have a friend with a large sea-faring yacht – it would have been great to use that to change the mindset of my team.'

So while the choice of venue for this two- or three-day event is important but not critical, do consider any opportunity to do something different – especially if you want to make a statement that you are going to make bold changes.

On a practical level, check you have the following:

- a room capable of seating twice the number of people as you have in the change planning team;
- daylight if possible, but not direct sunlight;
- air conditioning (if the weather is warm);
- access to a couple of smaller areas in addition to the main room, to use for teams of three or four in breakout sessions;
- a laptop with Excel;
- a flipchart, a new pad of A1 paper and pens;
- assorted stationery, such as Blu-Tack, folders, paperclips, plain paper, hole punch, pens, filing trays (desk trays that can hold A4 documents).

 Room checklist & Resources checklist

If possible, it is also a great help to have an administration person, who can ensure the smooth running of the sessions.

There are a number of other practical details to consider.

- **Timings**. Ideally start at 8.30 am and finish around 5.00 pm.
- **Refreshments**. Provide sufficient water, tea, coffee and food, so that the team is free to concentrate on the work required.
- **Dress code**. Preferably you should encourage a fairly smart rather than too casual appearance (for example, suit but no tie for the men) since this sets a tone that is professional and cohesive.

Step 9 summary

By the end of this step you will have:

- carefully prepared the logistics for the change planning session, to allow the change planning team to achieve the best result possible within an optimised working environment.

Step

10

Install fairness as a change driver

This step focuses on the critical factor of fairness when collecting the feedback.

The change framework outlined in this book is a rules-based framework. This has a number of advantages.

- For the **change planning team** the framework provides security, because all the team has to do is follow the well-defined rules.
- For the **businesses running the framework** the framework is learnable (because all rules are learnable) and therefore repeatable, so the framework is a good investment.
- For the **stakeholders and employees** the framework provides comfort and confidence, since the rules ensure that their input will be taken seriously and dealt with fairly.

The end of the period for the collection of Form1s is an opportunity to emphasise how the framework will treat the feedback fairly. You can make the most of this stage by following the suggestions listed below. The list may look like paranoia, but because of the emotional reaction of many people to the boxes it is essential to emphasise the fairness of the procedure.

- Make a public announcement in the area of the box that this box will close, and that any last input is now needed.
- Tape up the posting slot – make sure people are watching you when you do this.
- Tell people that the box is going straight to the venue where the change planning session will be held, or that it will be held in a neutral location under lock and key until this time.
- Hold all the boxes in the same location. Ensure this is not the CEO's office! Choose instead the post room, or a lockable meeting room.

- Inform people of the date of the change planning session, and tell them that full feedback will be announced to them within 48 hours of this work being completed.
- In each work area thank people for their input and views – this is common courtesy and costs nothing.

Step 10 summary

By the end of this step you will have:

- emphasised the importance of fairness in the actions presented, to make sure that performance and responses will be the best that they can be: this step is like putting oil into the engine.

Step

11

Conduct the change planning session

This step focuses on the first stages of the change planning session. The whole change planning session will require two or three consecutive days, depending on the number of Form1s submitted.

Because this framework is rules based it is important not to pervert a rule, change step or discard 'unwanted' bits. The rules are based on real people and follow a tried and tested approach: even if they appear strange or a little obvious, you need to follow them carefully, otherwise you will waste all the great effort that has been invested so far in this process.

There are four main stages in the change planning session.

- **Stating objectives**. The programme sponsor sets the foundation by reading the keynote speech.
- **Facing the issues**. The red boxes are emptied and the Form1s are read and filtered.(These two stages are set out in Step 11.)
- **Recommending action**. Syndicate groups suggest change projects for improvement, and a list is agreed by the whole change planning team. (This stage is set out in Step 12.)
- **Populating each project**. The team agrees information for each action programme. (This stage is set out in Step 13.)

Stating objectives

The change programme sponsor (the CEO or other business leader who is responsible for initiating the framework) starts the process by reading the prepared keynote speech.

The purpose of this stage is to:

- state the objectives and define the intended results;
- offer encouragement and support for the team.

Facing the issues

The red boxes containing the employee and stakeholder views are now opened for the first time, and spread into as many roughly equal piles as there are team members. The team then reads and organises employees' views – the planning issues on the Form1s.

The purpose of this stage is to:

- formally recognise the factors that make up the situation facing the team (past, present and future);
- lay the foundations for defining the required actions.

READING THE FORMS

The Form1s are opened, spread out and then read in silence. It is important to enforce the discipline of silent reading because then every view and every piece of information is given time: the data is 'internalised' without discussion, ridicule, qualification or rejection. Each team member then places their initials on each Form1 they read, to register the process (but not to agree or disagree with the content).

This is usually a sobering time for the team, as this will be the first time that many of them face the issues of the company as a whole – undiluted, unchanged and not distorted by interim management layers.

At this stage the team can also tally up the Strengths, Opportunities, Faults and Threats (SOFT) boxes on the Form1s. If a form does not have this box filled in, they can make a judgement, but they cannot change a pre-recorded tick. They then report back on the number of forms in each category.

It will now be possible to:

- count the total number of forms as a response indicator;
- show the 'sense' of the business as it reports itself – no interpretation is required.

 ## *SOFT analysis spreadsheet*

It can also be useful to compare your results with the average 'norms' of these first sessions:

- Strengths: 7%
- Opportunities: 9%
- Faults: 76%
- Threats: 8%

If you have done the communication bit right, and your response is more positive in the 'O' category, then congratulations!

USING A BUSINESS FILTER

The next task is to resolve this emotional content into a business filter. The business filter is a filing system for every Form1. (Remember, one of the rules is that no Form1 is ever discarded, no matter what it says.)

 ## *Business filter*

The filter can quickly be set up by using the filing trays recommended in Step 9. Label them as follows:

- **Product/service**. What it is and how it works, and when and where to make improvements.
- **Process**. How it will be made and/or assembled, subcontracting and purchasing, and labour and machinery.
- **Customers**. Who will buy it and how they can be persuaded to purchase the product.

- **Distribution**. How the product/service will be stored, transported and delivered.
- **Finance**. Where the money will come from and how the cash flow will be controlled.
- **Administration**. How the company will be managed, the management style, the organisation structure and the people-skills needed.

Each planning issue (Form1) is taken by a team member, and one by one they read out the title and give sufficient information so that the whole team can vote on where the Form1 belongs in the filter. It is not critical to get this perfectly right, since the process is flexible enough to account for any issues that end up in different trays.

This is the stage in the process where it is possible to bridge any perceived gaps between the front-line workforce and the management of the company. Invite a union representative to this part of the session and ask them to act as silent observers. Additionally or alternatively, invite workforce representation to observe the process.

Above all, it is important to emphasise that the contents of the Form1s are treated fairly – just as you promised. For my clients I provide a video recording of these two first stages above, using a camera on a tripod in the corner of the room. It acts as an audit tool if ever required, and demonstrates the absolute fairness of the process, showing how every Form1 is accepted and treated with respect.

ANALYSING THE FORMS

Once the filter is complete, it is time to move on to the working part of the session.

For this, you need to draw a grid on a flipchart, which lists the change manager's names and the six titles of the filter. What you need to do is to assign people to each filter team, but ensure they are not working in the filter team that encompasses their day job or primary responsibilities. You are in fact forming a 'lay team' – a team of *un*competence (as opposed to *in*competence!).

This is the unbiased team described earlier (Chapter 3). It makes it possible to comment across the organisation as a change manager and not as a functional specialist. For example, you would not assign the sales or marketing managers to look after the Customer filter, and you would not assign a human resources manager to review the Administration filter.

Recommending action

These syndicated groups will then move on to recommend action and the full team will decide which programmes will be implemented (Step 12).

Step 11 summary

By the end of this step you will have:

- set up a change planning session, following the rules and using the forms from the website;
- created the bones of the change plan, upon which you will now hang the clothes – the real plans;
- completed the stakeholder engagement, knowing it was the deepest audit of your company that is possible.

Step

12

Use your entire staff to extend your plan

This step focuses on creating a fully inclusive, strategy-focused list of improvement projects.

With the Form1s received from the workforce (including the directors and managers) it is possible to find common threads and issues. These can now be brought together to sit under a single title of **recommended action**. The purpose of this stage is to:

- permit an objective and candid determination of total requirements without embarrassing or threatening responsible individuals;
- produce a comprehensive list of actions covering all aspects of the operation.

Recommending action

Give your unbiased (syndicate) teams some working space in a breakout room or an alternative working area, to ensure they have privacy. They then work out a title of recommended action, which they record on a Form2a, which is clipped to the front of all the Form1s that have been used to reach that decision.

 Form2a: Recommended action

At this stage the syndicate teams should check that they have not omitted any area or subject. If there is something that still needs attention, for which there is no Form1, then they can use a Form2a action title with no forms behind it.

It may be helpful to have external facilitation in this part of the day, in order to test the discussions of the teams, add comments or ask questions, and ensure that the action title is strategically aligned to the keynote speech of change that drives this session.

Remember that all action titles need to be strategic as opposed to operational. For example, there is little point in taking the Form1s that relate to broken assets or repairs needed on buildings and simply deciding that the outcome action is to send out a contractor to fix them. What happens when something else breaks in three weeks' time? Instead, this is an opportunity to put a facilities management process in place to accept, report and fix all future issues.

Each syndicate team takes one filter and works on it until complete. Some teams may form and reform around the different filters. When I facilitate these sessions I usually assign a team of three or even four out of around ten managers to look at the Administration and Process piles, which are usually the largest and most complex. The other filters can be managed by just two or three people.

As the work progresses it may take up more time than suggested, so teams can be reassigned for efficiency, rather than waiting for a single person to become free from another filter. At all times, remember the concept of an unbiased team.

However, the six-business-filter allocation is not critical, and approximate assignment can be sufficient. Remember too that if your syndicate teams have found a Form1 that clearly talks about another filter, then this form can be moved between syndicate teams during this part of the process.

Each syndicate team uses the A1 flipchart paper to record their action titles. I use one paper for each filter subject, and give each project a sequential reference number – so if the Administration filter is worked on then the projects will be called A1, A2, A3 etc. for ease of identification. (You can then use P for Products, PR for Process, C for Customer, D for Distribution and F for Finance.)

Once the discussions have concluded, and every Form1 has been allocated to a suggested project, then you can move to the next stage.

REVIEWING THE ACTION PLANS

The syndicate groups come back into the main room with the six A1 sheets (one from each syndicate team – one per filter). The sheets are hung around the room, using the Blu-Tack you ordered in Step 9.

Each syndicate team nominates a spokesperson, and then each filter sheet is reviewed in detail. The spokesperson stands in front of the sheet and reads out the proposed title. The whole change planning team is asked to vote whether to:

- accept the title;
- suggest wording changes to clarify the scope or intent of the action;
- amalgamate it with another proposed project – either within the same syndicate or across another team (it may well be that Process and Finance have come up with a similar idea using different source data forms, so identifying similar projects avoids duplication and wasted work);
- reject the title completely, whereupon the syndicate team will need to rethink how to use the Form1s.

At this stage a majority voting system applies, but discussion is allowed for as long as the timetable allows.

Once the final list of action plans has been agreed then you have consensus as to the plan.

Reaching consensus

I am always intrigued to watch for what I consider to be the 'tipping point' in these change planning teams. This is the point in the process when I become invisible as the facilitator and instead the action titles and the discussions are all 'owned' by the change planning team. By the time you reach this part of the process, tipping point will have been achieved.

 *Delphi*

The final list is recorded using the Excel file provided on the website – called Delphi. Delphi is a way to get a wide group of people to reach consensus without argument – which sounds nearly impossible in the space of just 30 minutes. Yet within this time the Delphi tool will allow your change planning team to reach consensus on the proposed order in which the projects should be delivered.

The process is to ask each individual – without discussion – to rank the projects from 1–n (n being the total number of actions). For example, if there are 36 actions then 1 is considered the most important project to the business, and 36 the least. The Delphi sheets can record this information and sort out the order for you at the click of a mouse.

Print out the results and hand them out to each manager. This action draws to a close the work stage above and acts as a closure point.

Taking responsibility

Using the flipchart project lists, you now ask for volunteers for the work projects. Each project must be:

- assigned to a change manager to drive the project in the business (this is not to be confused with 'doing' – the manager will put together a workplace team to assist them);
- led by one person only, although others can be involved.

Make sure that each change manager takes responsibility for an equal work share – this is not simply the same number of projects, as some will be quick wins while others may be far-reaching and extensive.

Step 12 summary

By the end of this step you will have:

- used the Form1 feedback from staff as the basis to create new ideas;
- formulated projects to improve the business.

Step

13

Build a high performance plan

This step focuses on creating a single unified vision.

The team now records all available information pertaining to each action programme. This sets the foundation for planning individual actions by:

- avoiding false starts that might happen due to ignorance of past work or the rediscovery of available information;
- recognising the interrelationships between actions and responsible managers;
- setting up the coordination required for efficient implementation;
- identifying areas of potential risk and where future acceptance and support is important for success.

Populating each project

Normally in a session involving many people there is a free flow of ideas, with discussion that moves around, over, under and away from the subject in hand. But here the rules are simple and the discussions are carefully managed.

- Each change manager will by now have taken control of the Form2as, attached to the supporting Form1s, and will hole-punch them and put them into their control binder folder.
- Information and comments are then transferred to Form2b, which is the new front control sheet for each project (the **proposed action plan**).

Form2b: Proposed action plan

- Taking turns, each change manager reads the name of the project. Then from each team member they request a single statement, comment, advice or 'pass' (if there is nothing to add). It is imperative that uncontrolled discussion does not break out, or otherwise time will slip away.
- Each comment is recorded on the control sheet (Form2b) for later reference, and this is repeated until all projects have been completed in this way. So Form2b summarises the project and the collective wisdom of the whole change planning team.

By inviting individuals to speak, each person can buy into each other's projects, offering support and insight. This process also prevents a free-for-all where the single gem can often be missed. Finally, all the information is recorded by the responsible manager.

Once this stage is completed, the transformation planning work is completed for the session. But make sure that the team knows this is the start and not the end of the programme, and that there is further work to be done in the next 48 hours.

You can now release what will be a very tired team!

Planning the timing

Here are a few tips to help you plan how much time to allow for the change planning session.

- Once you start this session, it must not be stopped.
- The reading of the Form1s will take between 1.75 and 3 hours, depending entirely upon the number of forms you have received and the reading speed of the slowest person.
- Each step must be completed before the team moves on. Do not try to start the next step with a subset of a team who are perhaps faster readers than others.

- The filtering process will take a further 1 or 2 hours.
- The work of the unbiased syndicate teams will take between 4 and 10 hours. Do not try to speed this up. This is the time when your team will have a lot of thinking to do, some creativity to find and uncertainty to overcome, so this must not to be rushed.
- The Form2b process of populating the projects needs tight facilitation and chairing to ensure 'general discussion' does not break out. Allow around 4 hours for this. Again, don't rush, as this step allows all managers to buy in for the second time and support one another.
- As a rough guide, a change planning session consisting of 9 change managers, 500 Form1s and good facilitation can be completed in 2 days.
- When you rerun this session in the months or years to come, the same team can reduce the time taken (because they are familiar with the process) by around 35–40 per cent.

Completing the change planning

This is a useful place to recap on your progress so far. Using the framework approach, you have now achieved the following:

- You have established the link between the **strategy** and the business operations when determining changes. This is a powerful link and will accelerate results in the short term.
- You **communicated** the strategy to all stakeholders – be they employees, contracted workers, customers, suppliers or partners. The scope is as wide or narrow as you want.
- You installed **fairness** into the proceedings by setting up a mechanism whereby the stakeholders could feed back their views and opinions in an unstructured way. The anonymity of the **feedback** stressed the fairness of the process and made it different, while the 4–6 week period gave people time to submit their views. By making this process unstructured, you allowed anything and everything that caused a blockage or raised an opportunity to be known to you.

- You chose, interviewed and selected a **change planning team** to take on the responsibility for establishing the detail of the changes, and to carry out the work associated with the change framework.

- You set up and ran four developmental **skills workshops** for this team, to move their thinking towards change and to provide them with the confidence to do something different.

- You then brought the stakeholder feedback and the change planning team together for a two or three-day **change planning session**.

- You followed the **rules** and processes that have a proven track record.

- You visibly managed the stakeholder feedback into a **business filter** and **unbiased** subteams, which led to suggested **change projects** for improvement.

- You then tested, de-duplicated and fine-tuned the suggestions to become a list of **agreed projects**.

- This list was put **in order** using the Delphi technique, and then single managers in the change planning team assumed **responsibility** for the actions to complete the project.

- The change planning team then populated each **project** in turn, to provide the project owner with support, information and ideas.

- The **final list** was published to the team and the session closed.

Step 13 summary

By the end of this step you will have:

- welded together the strategic aspirations of the business, the views of the workforce and stakeholders, creating one single unified vision;
- suspended the workforce psychology of self-service for a while, and empowered your elite team of change managers to drive the changes.

Step

14

Publish to accelerate your results

This step focuses on the importance of communicating the change plan.

Earlier I outlined the concept of distributive justice – the balance between what is put in and what is perceived to be taken out, which prompts the question: 'What's in it for me?' (see Chapter 2). Because the Form1 feedback mechanism is anonymous and therefore completely fair, you can suspend the distributive justice model – for a while.

When the team at the Stanford Research Institute realised this, they became very excited. After all, if you can find a way to stop people behaving for their own good, setting up personal agendas and comparing themselves constantly with others in the company, just how much more productive could the company be?

Certainly, this change framework greatly reduces the number of 'games that people play' and promotes team performance. The reason for this is that there is a real perception of fairness, because:

- everyone is able to 'have their say';
- people are protected by using anonymity;
- every Form1 is included and none is discarded;
- each change manager is given the time to read every form, and to consider its content;
- unbiased teams deal with the ideas and blockages;
- a process or rules is used to remove subjectivity and individual personalities from the result;
- the results are published to provide feedback and thanks to everyone involved.

Perhaps the results are not perfect for each individual – perhaps they do not get everything they want – but the whole workforce has spoken. Everyone has signed up to the process, and whatever the outcome, it is deemed **fair enough**.

To complete the circle, it is now important that you, as the project sponsor, publish the list of agreed projects and get it back to the entire stakeholder group – quickly.

Publishing the findings

Using the Delphi tool that was introduced in Step 13, the output is easy to structure. It is possible to print directly from this spreadsheet, but I would strongly suggest that you go a lot further.

- Explain to everyone in the organisation exactly what has just happened, emphasising the fairness of the process.
- Describe the projects in team talks and briefings.
- Bring the projects to life by publishing updates of all actions that result.
- Announce any quick wins, to remind everyone that something is happening and that things are changing.

So is this really the perfect way to get all stakeholders to leave their personal issues at the door and come together as a great high performance workforce? Not quite. The positive effects of the fair approach of the framework can only be achieved if you:

- ensure open and honest publication of the results;
- maintain the feeling of inclusion by focused communication.

Communication is now critical to prolong the positive psychological effect of the process. If you fail to communicate, you will bring back the idea of distributive justice ('What's in it for me?') very quickly. So, it is vital that you:

- communicate every update;
- talk about the change projects at every opportunity;
- promote teams to be involved in the next actions;
- celebrate every success as projects are delivered.

According to psychologists, this will give you around 100 days of full support. When else have you ever had enthusiastic support for a week, let alone three months?

By remaining enthusiastic and open to communication you will have a higher number of engaged employees – as opposed to the disengaged or those who are semi-engaged.

Step 14 summary

By the end of this step you will have:

- started the critical stage of communication;
- understood that you need to perpetuate worker support by concentrating on communicating effectively with them in the months ahead.

Step

15

Drive rapid execution

This last step focuses on how you manage the change through to completion. The elements that drive the execution of change are not unique to any framework. They are simply a combination of good management and leadership style – or just good management sense.

By using the change framework in this book you have by now:

- brought together strategy and operational change;
- fully engaged stakeholders and employees;
- enhanced the change planning team by skills training and the experience of the change planning session itself.

After the discussions in the change planning session, teams often refer to the process as:

- exciting
- exploratory
- different
- safe (through following the rules)
- outcome focused
- revealing.

Contrast this list with the feelings they have when they first read the feedback:

- sobering
- depressing
- intense
- shocking
- empowering
- visionary
- revealing.

What words would you use to describe your change planning session?

Almost everyone will agree that the process has been a revelation – taking unstructured feedback, honestly given, and converting it in such a short, intense period of time into useful, impactful, powerful projects for change and improvement. So by the time you reach Step 15 the gloom is replaced by a positive outlook, or even a feeling of euphoria.

Taking action

What should happen next?

- **Say 'yes'**. The results are published, as above, and your role at this stage is simply to say 'yes'. By doing so, you endorse the hard work of your team, and allow them to showcase this work within the organisation. You may have reservations about a small number of the projects, but just for now go with it. You are not agreeing to a budget, or an outcome, you are simply saying 'yes' to acknowledge the hard work and allow a project to start.
- **Formalise the action**. Form4 – an application for authority to continue – must now be completed, in order to bring about a formal relationship between you and the change manager. This confirms you are taking the project seriously and that you expect professional action.

 Form4: Request for authority to proceed

- **Scope the project**. The project – the thing you are saying 'yes' to – must now be scoped and assessed for resources and return on investment (ROI). This provides you with additional control points and allows you to view the project is a more qualified way.

Form3: Financial plan & Form3a: Project plan

- **Communicate with the change planning team**. Ask the team to update you on their individual projects as often as you see them. If they know you are interested and want to see this work done, they too will be interested in doing it.

- **Agree to a monthly formal change planning team meeting**. This must be different from any other meeting you may normally hold. You should attend yourself and ask the same questions of each change manager of each project:
  - What is happening?
  - When is it happening?
  - What is the budget?
  - What are the controls and timescale for completion?
  - Do you need any help or additional resources?

- **Involve everyone**. Make sure that the change manager is using the company's resources to reach out to all the employees and stakeholders, and is involving them in the project teams. As long as people are involved in this way, then the perpetuation of the positive attitude will prevail.

- **Control the project**. Use existing project control software at this stage – there is no need to reinvent the wheel.

- **Celebrate success or progress**. Communicate with the employees and stakeholders to show them how – as a consequence of their input – the project is delivering.

- **Talk about the framework**. If people can relate to and identify with concepts in the framework, they know how to refer to it in the future. The framework then becomes a repeatable and desirable part of the culture of your organisation.

Overcoming concerns

It is useful here to review some common questions.

- **What happens if the project covers work we are already thinking of or doing?** The great thing about this framework is that, if this is the case, it doesn't matter. The Form1 feedback can be revealed to the existing work stream or project team, which often lends a powerful dimension to its work. At the change planning session stage, the fact that the initiative is already under way will be known to the change managers, and so the project title can be to 'accelerate', 'expand' or 'enlarge' the existing programme. In this way information can be shared. However, the responsibility to report back to the change planning team review meetings remains – and must be stressed.

- **What happens if a change manager leaves the company, is moved, is sick or in any way leaves the team?** Make sure that the work is assigned to another person immediately, either on a temporary or permanent basis. Then ensure that you communicate this widely.

- **When does this programme get repeated?** Organisations usually repeat this programme either every six months or annually. The programme can also be used whenever a change is required within a smaller, defined area of the business. Remember, this is now your own framework, so you should apply it whenever you think the approach will produce superior results. The Form1s can be restricted to a smaller number of people, and the keynote speech of strategy and change can be narrowed to a specific issue or area. However, there should always be a strategic focus, and never simply an operational one.

- **When we repeat this, do we need to go through the workshops again?** Not if the team is largely unchanged. You can simply issue the keynote speech, make Form1s available, define the timetable and then run the change planning session itself.

- **Can we have more than one change planning team within the organisation?** Absolutely yes. If you want a rule of thumb, one change planning team can handle up to 1,500 stakeholders, using a three-day change planning session. Any more than this and the paperwork burden will be too great for a single team. So within this framework you can run multiple framework programmes at once across the company – or across its subsidiaries and associated organisations. In this case, the project lists created should be reviewed to ensure there is no duplication of effort, and the change planning teams should nominate spokespeople to attend such a meeting.

- **What happens when a project is completed?** If a project is acknowledged as 'closed and completed' then it is removed from the regular update meetings and the results are correlated. It is then possible to provide a return on investment (ROI) statement, plus a statement of benefit to the company. This second statement should be published and distributed to the wider stakeholder group immediately after completion of the project.

- **What happens a few months later, or does this just carry on?** The sponsor reviews individual and group progress. This monitoring will include evaluating the achievements made, recording revised actions, notifying team members and reporting routine progress to seniors. The work continues until the objectives are reached. Work then stops.

- **Is the process computerised – it seems to need a lot of paper?** If a process is to be inclusive, it needs to be accessible by everyone, which includes those in the workforce who do not access computers. Additionally, the act of writing something down and posting it can be an important cathartic action by the individual, which cannot be replicated in an electronic form. Although the Form1 is available online, this is an alternative and not the main access method. Since the rest of the process is about handling and dealing with people and their feedback, it is best done using hard copy. Some things just do not belong on spreadsheets and screens, because they de-personalise the content. This change framework is deliberately designed to be personal, which is what gives it its power.

- **Why do some of the steps appear to be repetitive?** Any activity that involves people is going to have an element of repetitiveness, whether it is the time you spent at school learning something new by rote, or instructing people how to use a decision-making matrix. In this framework each step has a purpose and must not be omitted or skipped in any way.

Step 15 summary

By the end of this step you will have:

- concluded all 15 steps to installing a framework for leading constant change;
- understood how important it is for the framework to be GRAIL compliant:
    - Governance in place, with a rules-based approach.
    - Repeatable by your team at will at any time.
    - Auditable – from inception to delivery.
    - Inclusive of all your stakeholders.
    - Led strategically.

part three

It's the results that count

5

How to get the results you deserve

Key points in this chapter:

- How to get the general business performance uplift.
- Why communication is critical to accelerate results.
- How to include your people for a lasting effect
- How to define results:
  - cashable
  - non-cashable
  - intangible benefits.

This framework will already have made significant positive improvements to performance within your organisation. By allowing people to have a voice in the change framework, you have:

- provided a sense of fairness, which in turn has suspended the idea of distributive justice – 'What's in it for me?'
- encouraged additional effort, through the attitude of contribution;
- lifted the personal performance of individuals.

Getting fast results

So, you have just completed a change planning session that involved all your stakeholders. They are now waiting for some action. If you have followed the steps correctly, then by now you will have published the full list of developmental projects – this means the stakeholders have an idea of what should happen next.

On the list will undoubtedly be some **quick wins.** The clue is in the title – these must be achieved quickly. This then sends a message to all staff – that something is happening for a change. The good news for you is that quick wins usually cost little money, but gain a lot of applause.

What quick wins could you achieve in your organisation?

Many users of this framework report that these quick wins can be highly significant events and that profit and performance lifts are visible and measurable from these alone – before a single change project is started. But you will only benefit from such quick wins if you realise the importance of communication.

There is a tendency in human nature to revert to the old, known ways whenever there is a time of uncertainty. This is sometimes referred to as the **stress reaction** and typically it can manifest itself in two contrasting ways. For example, some people under stress may resort to repetitive behaviour: playing simple computer games over and over again, watching an old film they have watched many times before, retreating emotionally to a 'cave' and disconnecting. Other people might respond by over-communicating – they want to discuss the situation, unpick it and talk about it to others. Their instinct is often to reach out to others.

> *"At any given moment, we have two options: to step forward into growth or to step back into safety."*
>
> ABRAHAM MASLOW, AMERICAN PSYCHOLOGIST

If you fail to communicate the change plans and fail to continue to engage the workforce, then the idea of distributive justice will quickly replace all the good work you have done so far. Unless you give communication the attention it deserves, you will not get the result that you planned for in the previous steps. So it is critical that you as the programme sponsor are able to devote time and energy to promoting this aspect of communication and performance, and make sure that the appointed change planning team follows through.

Defining results

My most successful clients make sure that each individual in the change planning team knows that they are being measured by the outcome of the change projects, and that this will form a significant part of their performance appraisals. It is this direct link between a change programme outcome and the individual's appraisal that will ensure successful delivery of the change.

This chapter uses the word 'results' to describe the successful implementation of the change projects that your change planning team have begun. But just how do you go about measuring these results?

Cashable savings

First, there is the easy-to-understand financial saving or financial growth figure. This is easy to measure, as it can have a £, $ or € sign in front of it. It is real cash, because you can say, 'If I spend this, or I do this, then I can save or make x amount of money'. It is what I refer to as a cashable saving.

Some projects will fall into this category and are therefore easily measured.

Case study
Making cashable savings

At the end of a change planning session I had led with a packaging company, there was an exciting list of projects for improvement. Probably less than an hour after we had finished the session (in fact I was still packing away my resource box) one of the change planning team members returned to the room and announced he had just saved £35,000. His project

▶

was to create a formal supplier-and-purchasing framework. His first call had been to his pallet providers (they used hundreds of pallets per annum), and he told them that to retain the business they would need to review their prices. He then called other suppliers of pallets and in a short space of time had agreed a significant saving – approaching 18 per cent. This meant that his company immediately had a cashable saving of £35,000, which equated to £35,000 additional net profit. He was rightly delighted with this first quick win.

So why hadn't he done this before – why had he waited for a change planning session before using this idea? The simple truth was that he had never before been given the authority: the business had paid little attention to the obvious, and the directors were concentrating on growing sales and new customers rather than internal matters such as the price of pallets. Like many businesses, the incumbent supplier or situation will prevail as long as it is not perceived to be broken.

Non-cashable savings

A non-cashable saving is where you identify an efficiency that will show a saving – for example, by removing the human interface, or revising a process to save time. In this way you make capacity improvements, although you may not be planning (immediately) to convert this to a lower wage bill by reducing the number of people (which would then make this a cashable saving).

Very often Form1s refer to inefficient processes:

- Why does a process exist whereby three signatures are needed in different locations, causing huge delays?
- Why can't this be done like this instead, to save time and hassle?

These perfectly sound ideas are then acted upon, and processes are changed to make them more efficient and less expensive (all processes cost money). This reduces the **internal transaction** burden on your organisation.

Consider these figures, which show the different channels for transactions, and their comparative costs:

	FACE-TO-FACE	TELEPHONE	WEBSITE
Lower quartile average costs	£6.46	£1.08	£0.14
Median average costs	£7.81	£4.00	£0.17
Upper quartile average costs	£11.28	£6.35	£0.46

At first glance, your instinct might be to see how a channel shift could be used to save money – how you might automate a process and so release people from that task. You might make those people redundant, or redeploy them to other areas of the organisation that might need them. So decisions about communications channels will also relate to how people are deployed within the business. (But remember that sometimes transactions need 'people interaction', so replacing some channels with a computer may not always be a good idea.)

Case study
Making non-cashable savings

In a public sector organisation, many of the feedback forms were about the chaos of parking the vehicles needed every day – including small lorries, tractor lawnmowers, road sweepers and pavement sweepers. All this machinery needed parking and storing in a warehouse for overnight security. Due to varying shift times, these vehicles took nearly an hour a night to park in sequence. Then in the morning around half an hour was wasted while drivers waited for their vehicle to become accessible. There was a traffic jam every day. The obvious quick win for the senior change planning team was to organise this

▶

better. So with £30 of white paint and an assessment of vehicle and shift requirements, each person was allocated a parking slot and time window for their vehicle.

The result was instant. No longer did the work teams return to base an hour early, and no longer did they have to wait to start work on each shift. The new timings reduced the waste from 90 minutes a day to just 15 minutes: a total non-cashable saving of 75 minutes a day, equating to 375 minutes a week, which was around 1,500 minutes a month – equivalent to three days of productivity. Three days extra work each month on site, for no more money, for every worker involved. The work team numbered 23 people, so the result was astounding in its scope – but even more so in the simplicity. The cash-converted equivalent was around £36,000, but far more important was the improvement in morale. And all this by analysing the 'gripes' on the Form1s.

Intangible benefits

Many organisations have 'ways of doing things' that have built up over the years. This change framework encourages you to re-examine the 'old way' or 'normal way'. By using the framework, you will have an agreed number of projects that will start to change these constructs and change the way things are.

As human beings, it is sometimes the very little things in the environment that make a significant difference to the way we feel. If those small irks – those blockages that make no sense – are removed, and if people feel that management has finally 'listened and understand', then very often you can create a positive shift for very little effort or money.

Whenever I am facilitating a change planning session, if I see that a number of small quick fixes are possible then I suggest that the change planning team creates a single project, and wraps up half a dozen quick responses in that project. This project can be called 'Deliver quick wins'. The scope of these quick wins – the slight shift or even dismantling of the 'old' ways to create a desired 'new' way – is as varied as there are businesses. They can range from the seemingly trivial to the blindingly obvious, such as:

- revising the car parking regime
- changing time-keeping procedures
- reviewing holiday booking systems
- improving the upkeep and cleanliness of offices and factories
- fixing broken doors
- upgrading security
- supporting lone workers
- organising a Christmas party
- changing the dress code
- reallocating key holders.

The list is endless, but all these changes can have an impact. You can easily spot the things that are entirely reasonable and can be easily fixed. These may well have a knock-on effect on some financial measure, or make an eventual saving, but at this stage you should be more concerned to highlight what can easily and inexpensively be fixed in order to raise morale.

Case study
Achieving intangible benefits

One of the more unusual intangible projects I have witnessed in recent years was in a multicultural workforce. A large number of Form1s had been returned relating to unreasonable smoking breaks, and an equally large number requested a prayer room – somewhere that people could go to for their 10-minute prayers, three times a day (in keeping with their beliefs). It was interesting that the change planning team found it easy

▶

to discuss the issue of smoking breaks, and suggest these be limited to 10 minutes, three times a day, but struggled with the concept of allowing non-smokers to have a space for 10-minute prayers, three times as day.

During the discussions it became clear that both issues affected morale. The outcome was the provision of a quiet room, in which there should be no electronic devices, talking or discussion. The rules of the quiet room were posted on the door. This solution was inclusive because it did not segregate the workforce by way of religion, yet it provided the space that had been requested. If 10-minute breaks were provided for everyone, then the individual could choose whether to use those breaks for smoking, praying or reading in silence. This was perceived to be as broadly fair as could be. The result – the change planning team had provided a very fair outcome, and morale did indeed improve.

Measuring the cost benefits

Is it possible to measure the cost benefit of raising morale? Perhaps you could assess how increased morale leads to increased productivity – for example, 1 per cent, which equates to a non-cashable saving of 1 per cent of the salary bill. But making such a link is tenuous, and could run the risk of instant challenge. It is better not to waste your time in this calculation conundrum, but rather simply appreciate how the change will have a 'people' benefit.

However, it is important that you keep a running tally of the projects, which will include:

- the anticipated benefit as the project unfolds;
- the type of result – cashable or non-cashable savings, or simply an intangible benefit.

Every project should have a defined benefit statement attached to it in order to drive the direction and focus of the project itself, and allow you, as the sponsor, to assess, monitor and eventually measure the outcome. If a project does not have a benefit statement, then why bother doing it at all?

 ## *Benefit realisation record*

As well as the benefit statement on the website, you could also use the project management tools you already have as part of your standard reporting mechanism. Whatever recording method you use, this should be built into the review of project process as early as possible. Preferably a new record is produced and updated each month, so that:

- the **payback** concept is introduced early on (this is an important part of the new mindset – after all, return on investment (ROI) is what you are looking for);
- **estimating** returns becomes a process and not an immediate end result.

Unfortunately many managers hesitate at providing an initial best estimate because they do not want to be hung out to dry if it does not transpire. But the habit of estimating is a key skill for all managers, especially one who is dealing with change. You need to ensure that there will be no retribution if things do not turn out exactly as they suggested in the early days of the project. Instead you need to help people to develop the skill of estimating and forecasting, so that they can provide a running commentary on the project as it unfolds.

Celebrating success

Celebrating success is critical to successful communication – and yet so often it is overlooked or forgotten. Remember that you received feedback from the workforce and your stakeholders, and it was their input that led to a project that is results driven and worthy of attention. So when this project is complete, then you need to **publish** the result. Make an announcement, as and when it happens.

People like to see movement, progress, activity and validation of the work that has been created. In short, your stakeholders demand feedback and thanks – especially if you want to keep them engaged. It's important to them, so make it important to you as the change sponsor, and measure your change planning team on the effectiveness of their communication. Use a variety of channels of communication at different times to ensure understanding – remember the 7 × 7 matrix of communication (Step 3).

Including people in change

Results are best obtained – and made sustainable – through **inclusion**.

When the change planning team emerges from the change planning session, they will each have a number of projects assigned to them, and they are then asked to report back at four-week intervals until the project is completed. A common reaction is that these managers feel a sense of foreboding, as they believe the work now falls to them, adding yet more pressure to their workload. But this is not so.

There is always the opportunity to reach back into the business, and to form a project team of people who are able to help deliver the project. You should encourage the formation of such subteams so that other people are included in formulating the final solution – which includes the study, the work and the reporting necessary for the project. It is this very act of including others that will heighten engagement and mean that all the changes can be put in place more easily.

You need to stop trying to manage a project through directing, allocating and budgeting. Don't ask:

- How do I do it?
- When is it going to get done?
- Who's going to do it?

Instead, ask:

- Who wants to help make this happen?

- How would you do it?
- What are you willing to do to get it done today?

This is how you are able to motivate other people and generate greater impact of the change.

So when someone raises their hand, give them permission, give them protection and encourage them. When those people come to you to ask for something – a little help, a resource, or a budget – give it to them. Whatever their plan is to get it done, let them carry on.

As soon as two, three or four people start taking those first steps – and you make their effort public and visible – you show others what success looks like. People then won't just start to follow you; you'll see followers getting out in front of the leader – going in the direction you want them to go.

Action points

- Reward those who think with a new or energised approach.
- Welcome fresh ideas, however bizarre they may appear to be.
- Do not dismiss or ignore ideas in meetings.
- See challenges and problems as opportunities to improve, not as a means to beat people.
- Develop a system internally that allows reflective thinking, innovation, new ideas and new ways to do things.
- Remember that most of the answers to the questions you have will lie somewhere within your organisation – by adopting a culture of thinking, innovating, challenging the old and embracing the new, you can raise the chances of your own success considerably.
- Involve everyone in the work, so that you accelerate your business development and gain performance increases.

6

How to make change a habit, not just an event

Key points in this chapter:

- How to create leader managers in your business.
- How to encourage and install change thinking as an ongoing process.
- How to rerun the programme at your will.
- How to cement your gains into your business.

A **leader manager** is a manager within any business who is asked to step up in performance terms, to provide direct support to the directors. In most companies directors are preoccupied with the operational aspects of their businesses: 'Dragged into detail', as one of my clients described it. They are unable to separate the operations from the strategy. This, of course, is a mistake, because not only will it hold back the business performance, it will also take up huge amounts of directors' time, causing them or you to work longer hours, to your own detriment.

The structure to drive any change must therefore:

- lift the executive team into leading strategically;
- lift the management team to fill the void;
- enable all teams to contribute and engage;
- adopt a fairness-based working practice;
- discard unneeded initiatives;
- communicate massively;
- support the managers to manage.

The workload audit sheet from Step 8 emphasised the need for managers to 'step up' and lead strategically. Using the framework to install new change planning competencies will also create additional responsibilities and work profiles. The behaviours of your high-performance change planning team also need to be considered, and perhaps can form part of the discussion both before and also after the change planning session, to reinforce the new arrangements.

Remind your change planning team that they have already made a shift: by the very nature of the change planning work they have become generalists and no longer specialists. It is important that they:

- understand all aspects of the business;
- do not over-supervise their former specialist area;
- define the key performance indicators (KPIs) and test them for sanity;
- do not create new systems for the sake of it.

Boundaries are moving and resource points are shifting, which will give way to changing job roles and responsibilities. Flexibility is the key to success.

Getting into change thinking

Change is not a one-off event – it is a constant. Yet to have daily change activities introduced in your business would lead to uncertainty, chaotic approaches, unfinished plans and ultimately an inefficient operation. You need some rules.

Wherever people are involved, our psychology demands some surety and stability, or at least a level of understanding as to what is needed of us in our working lives. For that reason this framework operates using the building blocks of any organisation: **projects**.

People also need periods of time when they can draw breath and take stock of the current situation, which is why leading change on a daily basis would simply destabilise the business. So the change planning framework is designed to be operated on a **periodic** basis.

Most of my clients run a company-wide change planning session (as described in this book) on an annual basis. Some use it as the start of the annual planning process, and so create a process for refreshing the business plan and all their budgets. Others use it whenever change dictates, for example when there is:

- a restructure
- an acquisition or merger
- a new product or service
- a change of office
- a new leader.

Case study
De-risking an acquisition

A client had recently made an acquisition. His due diligence had looked at the financial position and the viability of bringing two finance reporting systems together, examined detailed contracts, analysed the customers, and of course interviewed the senior management team remaining with the business. Upon acquisition, however, a large number of people-related issues surfaced. The culture of the two companies was distinctly different, and this then led to a number of resignations of key people. The usual due diligence was not enough to foresee these obstacles. However, if the company had used the change framework it would have been able to head off, diffuse or constructively address the people issues and so might have achieved a much more positive outcome.

The interesting aspect of this framework is that the change projects continue to run, even when the Form1 collection process has ended. If you have successfully involved other people in the delivery of the projects, then the defined change is accessed by a team much larger than your appointed change planning team. This means that the thinking and the **change conversation** keeps on going, which is a great plus for you as the leader of constant change. You are therefore able to capture additional thoughts, ideas, and stimulate a positive approach to change as a culture.

What you must do is ensure all staff understand that they are now on a 'change train' that does not stop, except for these defined change planning events.

Creating a change-thinking culture

So just how do you achieve change thinking as a culture within your organisation? The answer is that you need to spread the use of this change framework throughout your business. It is not enough to create one change planning team, and run one change planning event (even if it includes everybody).

You need to empower more change planning teams, in all the sites or buildings, departments and subsidiaries. By using the same change framework, you will achieve a common, consistent, standard approach to building change into your organisational culture.

You have bought into a framework that is repeatable: so repeat it. Remember, this is not an isolated or simple initiative like those your business may have tried in the past. Instead, this is the cultural platform upon which all change can be planned and then played out.

- No longer will your staff engagement be a passive or neutral exercise. **It will now have power, purpose and measurable outcomes.**

- No longer will your management teams operate in silos and play politics with organisational resources. **They will now start to work together in one focused team or teams.**

- No longer will organisational structure prevent great ideas from reaching the board room. **There is now a process and framework for enabling the business.**

- No longer can individuals or departments cover up issues and ignore interdepartmental pressures. **This framework brings down the walls and overcomes the games people play.**

- No longer does the prospect of initiating and driving an organisational change hold such fear and resistance. **You now have the framework to do the job.**

Change thinking is your future, and will enable your organisation to make forward strides with confidence, instead of small steps with caution. Your role as the leader of constant change is to:

- install frameworks for change;
- hold on to the frameworks, resisting attempts to overcome them;
- use the collective power of your company's people to create a culture where there is only one direction – and that is forwards.

Action points

- Remember that leaders can be created at all levels in your organisation.
- Elevate your existing managers in your business.
- Take the lead in encouraging and rewarding change thinking – in every aspect of your company and at every level.
- Make sure that people realise this framework is not a one-off event – it is your new management system, which is capable of driving change and delivering results.

Conclusion

As you reach the end of the book, it is useful to recap the ideas behind the change framework and the steps you have taken.

Chapter 1 examined the global context of change, and why this acceleration of change is happening, due in most part to technology and rising global population as the primary drivers. It looked at the consequences if you just 'stay calm and carry on' – for any business in a competing or shifting market this is simply not an option.

Chapters 2, 3 and 4 set out the case for a defined framework for leading constant change – one that is GRAIL compliant (it has Governance in place, is Repeatable by your team, is Auditable, Inclusive and Led strategically).

The framework is deployed in just 15 practical steps:

1 You started the programme by redefining your strategy and direction via a **keynote speech**.
2 You selected and appointed a **change planning team**, responsible for adopting and delivering the work of this framework.
3 The strategy was **communicated** to all stakeholders.
4 You **engaged** your staff through feedback collected on anonymous Form1s.
5 You created a learning and exploration base through **four skills workshops**, which not only 'unstuck' management thinking, but also brought the team together as a ninja fighting force. The first of these covered **leading change**.
6 The second workshop emphasised the importance of **understanding finance**.
7 The third workshop looked at **project planning**.
8 The fourth workshop explored **how organisations really work**.

9   You prepared the **environment** for the change planning session, to allow the change planning team to achieve the best results.

10 You made sure that everyone was aware of the defined rules of the framework and the concept of **fairness**.

11 You brought the change planning team and the feedback data together in a **change planning session** that involved just two or three days of time.

12 Your change planning team used feedback to produce **ideas** for change projects.

13 Your change planning team created a fully inclusive, strategy-focused list of **improvement projects**.

14 You **published** these projects to all stakeholders to complete the circle of trust.

15 You supported the **delivery** and communicated success of the work through to completion.

This change process – which creates developmental ('change') work in project form, with ROI statements and formal work plans – can be a great way to appraise your management teams. You can use it to determine promotions, plan for succession and even create a formal leadership development programme.

The change planning framework allows you to assess and develop people both in terms of their membership of the change planning team, but also as part of the working parties established after the change planning session, which carry out identified and authorised work. One of my clients recently told me that they were discontinuing their own 'Leadership and management' training programmes, which used external venues and single chalk-and-talk courses. They were opting instead for this framework, which is based on the real work of the company. It also pays for itself, as opposed to being a management training cost.

Leading change

As you begin your own change journey, remember these important points.

- Change in your business is **inevitable** and is happening right now, whether you know it (and like it) or not.
- Change that is **unmanaged** can cause businesses to fail with little notice, or just fail over time.
- The **drivers** for change are both external (various big factors such as technology and global trade shifts) and internal (your own people, and products and services).
- An understanding of **finance** is essential to protect your business, and also to plan to transition through change.
- Your own **people** can enable or disable changes, despite your best efforts.
- **Inclusion** is therefore critical to change thinking and change acceptance.
- People psychology is often too inaccessible for the workplace, but adopting a tried and tested framework is **practical** and can optimise results.
- You need a **change planning team** that is specifically tasked to initiate and drive the change framework.
- A **rules-based framework** provides security during transition – with more accurate and faster planning, a focus on strategy and measurable outcomes.
- **GRAIL** compliance is not just a description, it is a philosophy.
- **Fairness** is a key driver for performance, providing a systematised way to achieve results.
- Efforts at staff **engagement** are only effective if they encourage active engagement.
- Linking operations to **strategy** provides a powerful energy for success and a focus going forwards, as opposed to simply being very busy in the daily operations.
- Joining strategy to operations requires meaningful,

measurable work that is **relevant** to all staff and stakeholders – this framework provides the project-by-project building blocks to make this link.

 Will you now take action to lead constant change, or will you choose to do nothing – and risk everything?

Online resources

Leading Constant Change is not simply about reading a book. You have just joined a community of business leaders who are all experiencing similar issues and questions in their own organisations. Whatever the size of your company, from very large to very small, and whatever your products or services, you share the same agenda and ask the same question: 'How can I lead to succeed, in a constantly changing environment?'

To help you, I have provided not only a book but also an active website and links to a real team of support professionals.

The website

 www.managingconstantchange.co.uk

Wherever you see the website content icon, then you can go to the website, navigate to the chapter and find the file relating to this section. In exchange for your email address, you can download material and use it for your own purposes. The content is split into chapters, so that you can simply click on the chapter link and access the support materials. I have used standard PDF format as downloads, so you will need to install a PDF reader on your computer or tablet.

The website provides forms and tools used in the framework. The forms are self-explanatory, but if you need to clarify any aspect then you can contact me or my team directly at: **support@managingconstantchange. co.uk**

You will also find a bonus chapter that outlines five key things that will ensure your success in the decade ahead – and the consequences of ignoring them.

Ongoing support

If you sign up on the website you will also receive:

- notifications of any updates of the forms or content on the site;
- blogs, articles and links to commentaries.

Once you have assembled your change planning team, get them to sign up as well, and treat them each to a copy of this book!

In many change programmes, the value of using external facilitation is well recognised, so there is also a section on the website that can introduce you to professionally trained practitioners, with whom you can discuss external help, training or facilitation.

LinkedIn

To support you even more, there is a LinkedIn Group called Leading Constant Change that can be found by searching the Groups, or by going to:

www.linkedin.com/groups?home=&gid=7415375

Please feel free to join this group and take part in live discussions with other readers. This is a true community of professional change planners, where you can exchange ideas, questions and views as you wish.

About Team Action Management

The change framework outlined in this book is built on a programme called Team Action Management (TAM). It was developed out of the work of the Stanford Research Institute in the 1960s, and publicised through Planning Seminars between 1964 and 1970. In 1971 Albert Humphrey, who then owned the patent to the process, came to the UK at the request of the Hambledon family (who owned W.H. Smith & Son). During the next 34 years 'Humph' delivered TAM to many household corporates in the UK and Europe, until his death in 2005. The intellectual property, patents and trademarks are now owned by TAM UK.

One of the key attributes of this framework is that it is simple in its application, despite being based upon complex and joined-up psychology and thinking. The diagram shows why the framework is so efficient and why it works every time. The reason is simply because it accommodates human psychology and people. After all, it is people not processes who innovate, drive your business, and do extraordinary things in pursuit of your success. It is people who differentiate your business from other businesses, and it is people – with all their issues, baggage and preconceptions – who will either reject or accept the plan for change.

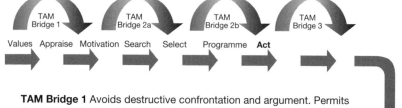

TAM Bridge 1 Avoids destructive confrontation and argument. Permits the group to tackle all issues without agreement on basic values.

TAM Bridge 2a Makes possible actions recommendations without being blocked by negative attitudes or lethargy.

TAM Bridge 2b Permits the individual to accept improvements in his own area without feeling embarrassed, threatened by recrimination or confessing to incompetence. Permits creative fresh look.

TAM Bridge 3 Reinforces individual commitment to produce result. TAM work is created. Self-imposed objectives and controls to planned schedule and budget are agreed.

How TAM drives change

- **TAM bridge 1 (Form1).** Employees, managers, directors and all stakeholders are invited to submit as many Form1s as they want, to highlight planning issues. The anonymous aspect and the pre-recording of the process makes it possible to consider each and every submission fairly, without the usual discussion, discrimination, discarding or discrediting of any single view. Using Form1 avoids destructive confrontation and argument and allows the group to tackle all the issues without having first to agree on basic values.

- **TAM bridge 2a (Form2a).** This form is used in the change planning session to record the suggested titles made by the unbiased teams. It allows recommendations to be made that are not blocked by negative attitudes or lethargy – it removes preconceptions and any risk of ideas and views being dismissed.

- **TAM bridge 2b (Form2b).** Used in the change planning session, this form allows the team to support each other's projects in a fair and supportive manner. Individuals realise that the team is operating as a whole across all areas, and so they can accept improvements in their own area without feeling embarrassed – they do not feel threatened by recrimination or feel that they have to confess to incompetence. So it allows a creative, fresh look at issues.

- **TAM bridge 3 (Form3, Form3a and Form4)**. These forms provide a strong project management approach to getting a result, and are supported by regular review meetings that ensure forward movement in every project. They reinforce individual commitment, since self-imposed objectives and controls to schedules and budgets are agreed. Eventually it will be possible to provide statements of benefit and to publish regular updates and results to all stakeholders.

The reason why the TAM framework drives change is that it takes into account the human decision-making process. All too often, differences in values, ability, motivation and creativity slow down a team that need to make a decision. By using the TAM framework, it is possible for the team to work towards a focused and agreed outcome.

The TAM framework allows you, as the business leader, to skim over (like a flat stone across the pond) the people behaviour that usually slows down and derails other change programmes. The framework uses the knowledge of your own people to harness the best, using the concept of fairness. It is a truly simple yet powerful approach, backed by science and provable results.

Clients of Team Action Management

The following comments, from CEOs and change directors who have all used the TAM framework, will give you some examples of the framework in action.

> *"Very effective tool to support the process of transitioning a large team from a public sector client to arvato UK, a private business. Using TAM, arvato was able to engage with our new employees early on, effectively managing change, while providing evidence of the measurable impact that it is having on the business."*

JOHN WYBRANT, KEY ACCOUNT DIRECTOR, ARVATO
(PART OF BERTELSMANN GROUP)

"TAM was a great help for integrating Kier Property Maintenance and colleagues from the Facilities Management of Sheffield City Council property portfolio. It helped the workforce of mixed blue and white collar to make a smooth transition from a public to a private, commercial mindset. TAM provided 'buy in' and 'trust' to employees entering a workplace with a totally new culture."

MARK STEED, DIRECTOR, KIER ASSET PARTNERSHIP SERVICES
(PART OF KIER GROUP)

"TAM has returned both savings and additional revenue, brought about by new idea exploitation equal to many times its cost in a very short time."

ANDREW FRITH, GROUP CEO, WFO GROUP

"TAM helped us find out what our staff think, and challenged us to act upon honest feedback. This resulted in a number of projects which have and will continue to bring our business real value. They will also deliver on to our bottom line. TAM was great at keeping the projects moving and keeping us focused on seeing them through to conclusion ensuring we attained maximum value."

PAUL DICKSON, MANAGING PARTNER, ARMSTRONG WATSON
ACCOUNTANTS

"The City of Edinburgh Council opted for the TAM approach to staff engagement as it offered a unique package in terms of its structure, component elements, and delivery timeframe, and fitted well with the Council's internal change methodology."

JENNIFER WILSON, CUSTOMER SERVICE MANAGER, CITY OF
EDINBURGH COUNCIL

The list of organisations that have used this TAM framework is impressive. From small businesses to the largest of listed companies, regardless of sector or product, the framework has been used to merge, acquire, restructure and achieve cultural integration, and to initiate and drive changes.

TAM client list

These companies all have just one thing in common: they recognise that sustainable change, where people are involved, requires a robust framework. So now you know that you can join this elite club of users and install this framework with confidence. Whether you are driving profit or service, growth or survival, you need the rules-based framework that TAM provides.

What did you think of this book?

We're really keen to hear from you about this book, so that we can make our publishing even better.

Please log on to the following website and leave us your feedback.

It will only take a few minutes and your thoughts are invaluable to us.

www.pearsoned.co.uk/bookfeedback

Index

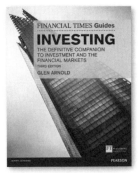

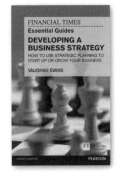

Do you want your people to be the very best at what they do?

Talk to us about how we can help.

As the world's leading learning company, we know a lot about what your people need in order to be better at what they do.

Whatever subject or skills you've got in mind (from presenting or persuasion to coaching or communication skills), and at whatever level (from new-starters through to top executives) we can help you deliver tried-and-tested, essential learning straight to your workforce – whatever they need, whenever they need it and wherever they are.

Talk to us today about how we can:

- Complement and support your existing learning and development programmes
- Enhance and augment your people's learning experience
- Match your needs to the best of our content
- Customise, brand and change it to make a better fit
- Deliver cost-effective, great value learning content that's proven to work.

Contact us today:
corporate.enquiries@pearson.com

ALWAYS LEARNING

PEARSON